HSK 2 Chinese Grammar

HSK 2 Chinese Grammar

A Chinese Grammar Wiki Book

Editor-in-Chief John Pasden

Foreword by Dr. David Moser

SHANGHAI

Published by AllSet Learning, Shanghai, China.

For information about educational or bulk purchases, please contact AllSet Learning at sales@allsetlearning.com.

1st print edition, 2019.

Paperback ISBN: 978-1-941875-45-2
eBook ISBN: 978-1-941875-46-9
ASID: 20190622T231110

For anyone who needs to pass the HSK
but also wants to *really learn* Chinese
and get a solid grasp of its grammar.

Table of Contents

Foreword

Learning Chinese used to be a frustratingly "front-loaded" endeavor. One had to first learn pinyin, the four tones, how to write thousands of characters with the correct stroke order, how to use the 214 radicals to look up unfamiliar characters in a dictionary, and, of course, how to limn the mysterious principles of Chinese grammar. This process entailed inordinate sacrifices of eyesight, friends, and years of precious life spent "learning to learn Chinese," before the hapless student could be weaned from a diet of pre-digested pabulum and delve into the messy, glorious world of real texts.

The Chinese Grammar Wiki is on the cutting edge of a growing arsenal of digital and web resources that have made this front-loaded Sisyphean nightmare a thing of the past. This very cool tool, developed by John Pasden and the folks at AllSet Learning, is in accordance with the new "learning grammar as you go" principle of Chinese study in the digital age. Learners can now boldly embark on the ocean of Chinese very early on, with navigational tools like the Grammar Wiki to reduce the risk of getting lost at sea. For the intrepid, motivated learner, studying Chinese can now be an adventure, instead of a five-year stint in solitary confinement. And from the very outset, students can begin to move toward the goal that was formerly so elusive: the acquisition of 语感 (yǔgǎn), the "feeling for the language."

In my opinion, the Chinese Grammar Wiki has at least three very strong characteristics:

Modularity. This is a long-standing commonsense feature of website design, but it's absolutely crucial for a grammar tool like this. The Wiki has conveniently carved up Chinese grammar into useful modular chunks with the beginner in mind, so that searching for a structure or topic is intuitive, quick, and yields a clear explanation that enables the user to forge ahead, enlightened and empowered. The structure and site map is user-friendly at every level, which means that the Wiki can be easily "plugged in" to existing Chinese syllabi, or simply employed by the student independently to explore texts and materials outside of class.

Interlinking. The Wiki is structured so that alongside the grammar points on most pages there are helpful links to related or similar grammar points within the Wiki. For example, in exploring the grammatical points for 比 (bǐ) involving comparison, you will find explanations of the basic 比 (bǐ) structure, examples, and common errors, but in addition you will also see links to other "comparison" structures using 没有 (méiyǒu). This interlinking feature gives the user a fuller picture of various grammatical structures that serve similar functions in the language.

Universality. One of the strongest points of the Chinese Grammar Wiki is that the grammatical explanations have been tailored so as to contain the right amount of information, at the right level of specificity and complexity for the majority of learners. Designing a grammar resource with such wide applicability is not an easy task, requiring not only technical know-how and careful thinking, but also a strong intuitive sense of what the average student needs to know. Linguist Edward Sapir said "all grammars leak," and this mutable, watery quality of language means that no grammatical framework is going to contain only tidy, airtight rules that cover every situation. In explanations, there is always a tradeoff between succinct simplicity and the real-life complexity, and the Wiki does an admirable job of striking a satisfying balance between these two yin-yang poles.

Being digital in nature, the Chinese Grammar Wiki is very much a work in progress, and the designers always welcome input and suggestions. Product development is always an interactive process, and the more people use the resource, the more useful it will become. I encourage Chinese students at all levels – and even Chinese teachers – to check it out and discover what the reference tools of the 21st century will look like.

No matter what well-meaning pedagogical Pollyannas might tell you, Chinese is still "damn hard." Thankfully, there now are digital resources like the Chinese Grammar Wiki, which goes a long way to making the struggle easier.

David Moser
Academic Director, CET Beijing Chinese Studies
Beijing Capital Normal University

Introduction

The **Chinese Grammar Wiki** began life as an Excel spreadsheet full of grammar points organized by difficulty level. This list was needed to track the progress of AllSet Learning's clients and to design personalized grammar practice where it was most needed. But as the lists continued to grow and evolve, it quickly became apparent that it made sense to put the grammar points online, so that the newest version would always be front and center. For ease of editing, what could be better than a wiki? And if AllSet Learning teachers were to have access, why not open up access to *all learners*? The Chinese Grammar Wiki was developed internally for about a year before becoming public in January of 2012. Since then, it has grown tremendously, both in content and in traffic.

Probably the most important feature of the Chinese Grammar Wiki, which has always been kept at the forefront of its development, is its focus on learner level. An absolute beginner can't absorb a multitude of uses for every grammar point she encounters, and she shouldn't be expected to. And she certainly shouldn't be given frustratingly difficult example sentences when trying to grasp the most basic grammar concepts. That's why example sentences on the Chinese Grammar Wiki are plentiful, but relentlessly edited to be level-appropriate. And for the learners that can't get enough, relevant articles of all levels are always just a link away. Although the wiki aims to be 100% comprehensive, it's no coincidence that there are fewer A1 grammar points than A2 grammar points, and fewer A2 grammar points than B1 grammar points. Considerable thought and care has gone into curating and pruning the lists of grammar points.

The Chinese Grammar Wiki is not a Chinese course. Rather, it is a companion resource that can complement any Chinese class. Don't expect to read it from start to finish, or to go through the grammar point lists from top to bottom. But do expect to come back often. And expect to get sucked into the curiously logical world of Chinese grammar.

John Pasden
Editor-in-Chief and CEO
AllSet Learning, Shanghai, China

HSK Levels and CEFR Levels

Since the company's inception in 2010, AllSet Learning has used the Common European Framework of Reference (CEFR) levels for its clients and study materials. CEFR has a great reputation for being practical and descriptive of communicative proficiency (we especially like the "Can Do" statements) while mercifully keeping the leveling and sub-leveling to a minimum. The A1-A2, B1-B2, C1-C2 progression is intuitive and helpful for both learners and educators, and can also be fairly easily converted to the American ACTFL level system.

The current version of the HSK (*Hanyu Shuiping Kaoshi*) dates back to 2010, and was last revised in 2012. It consists of six levels (1-6), and was designed, in part, to correspond to the six CEFR levels. European Chinese language teachers have reported that the correspondence, in practice, is somewhat different, with HSK 6 actually matching no higher than the CEFR B2-C1 level range. Furthermore, the HSK levels are used more as a standard for academic requirements (e.g. being admitted to an undergraduate or graduate program in China) rather than real-life application (the above-mentioned "communicative proficiency").

Our conclusion is that while both leveling systems clearly have their uses, it is not possible to equally accommodate both systems in one list of grammar points. That is why the Chinese Grammar Wiki has created separate listings for CEFR levels and HSK levels. We encourage test-takers of the HSK to refer to the HSK level lists, while learners focused more on real-life communication can benefit more from the CEFR levels. This book focuses on the HSK levels.

Continuation with "hai"

Although 还 (hái) has many meanings, the basic meaning of "still" to indicate a continuing action is essential to mastery of the word.

Affirmative Form

Usage of 还在

Often the auxiliary verb 在 (zài) will appear with 还 (hái), as it is natural to talk about *continuous* actions that are *still* happening.

Structure

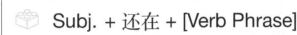

 Subj. + 还在 + [Verb Phrase]

Examples

- 这件事情我 还在 考虑。
  Zhè jiàn shìqing wǒ hái zài kǎolǜ.
  I am still thinking over this matter.
- 已经中午了，他 还在 睡？
  Yǐjīng zhōngwǔ le, tā hái zài shuì?
  It's already noon and he's still sleeping?
- 她 还在 生气吗？
  Tā hái zài shēngqì ma?
  Is she still mad?
- 你怎么 还在 用那个旧手机？
  Nǐ zěnme hái zài yòng nàge jiù shǒujī?
  How come you're still using that old cell phone?
- 你 还在 玩游戏？明天不是有考试吗？
  Nǐ hái zài wán yóuxì? Míngtiān bù shì yǒu kǎoshì ma?
  You're still playing video games? Don't you have an exam tomorrow?

Usage of 还是

Here 还是 (háishì)–not literally "still is"–indicates what happened or will happen, *despite* the situation. The 是 (shì) here doesn't have a clear meaning here independent of 还 (hái).

Structure

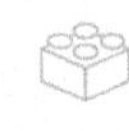

……，(但是 / 可是 +) Subj. + 还是 + [Verb Phrase]

Examples

- 我让他不要买，他 还是 买了。
  Wǒ ràng tā bùyào mǎi, tā háishì mǎi le.
  I told him not to buy it, but he still bought it.
- 他不想离婚，但是最后 还是 离婚了。
  Tā bù xiǎng líhūn, dànshì zuìhòu háishì líhūn le.
  He didn't want to get divorced, but in the end he still ended up getting divorced.
- 父母不同意他去，可是他 还是 去了。
  Fùmǔ bù tóngyì tā qù, kěshì tā háishì qù le.
  His parents didn't agree to it, but he still went.
- 医生不让她喝酒，她 还是 喝。
  Yīshēng bù ràng tā hējiǔ, tā háishì hē.
  The doctor told her to stop drinking, but she still drinks.
- 老师生病了，但是她 还是 来上课了。
  Lǎoshī shēngbìng le, dànshì tā háishì lái shàngkè le.
  The teacher is sick, but she still come to class.

Negative Form

Structure

When you put 不 or 没 after 还 (hái) in a question sentence, it can be used to emphasize the idea of what *should* be happening in a more idiomatic way.

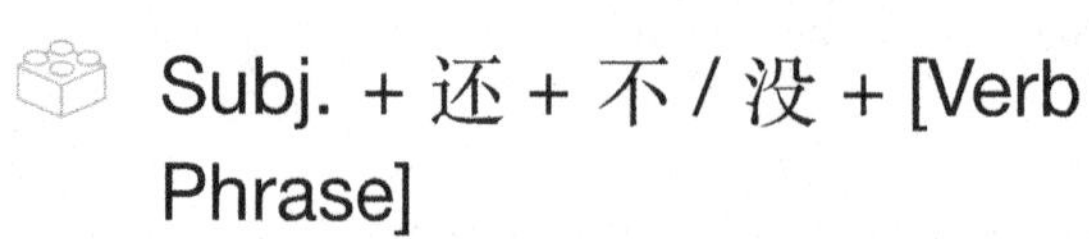

Subj. + 还 + 不 / 没 + [Verb Phrase]

Examples

- 我们等了半个小时了，老师 还没 到。
  Wǒmen děng le bàn gè xiǎoshí le. Lǎoshī hái méi dào.
  We've been waiting for half an hour, but the teacher still hasn't arrived.
- 电影已经开始了，你 还没 出门？
  Diànyǐng yǐjīng kāishǐ le, nǐ hái méi chūmén?
  The movie has started already, and you still haven't left the house?
- 你已经四十多了，还不 想结婚？ *implying the listener should get married now*
  Nǐ yǐjīng sìshí duō le, hái bù xiǎng jiéhūn?
  You're in your forties, and you still don't want to get married?
- 我解释了这么多遍，你 还不 懂？
  Wǒ jiěshì le zhème duō biàn, nǐ hái bù dǒng?
  I've explained it so many times, and you still don't get it?
- 我对你这么好，你 还不 高兴？ *implying the listener shouldn't be so upset*
  Wǒ duì nǐ zhème hǎo, nǐ hái bù gāoxìng?
  I treat you so well, but you're still not happy?

Similar to

- Expressing "and also" with "hai" (HSK2), page 26
- Moderating positive adjectives with "hai" (HSK2), page 48
- Advanced uses of "hai" (HSK5)

Emphasis with "jiushi"

As an adverb, 就 (jiù) can be placed before the predicate to add emphasis. It often has an intense or provocative feel to it, similar to "just." In English we might say, "it's *just* not right!" This emphasis very often appears as 就是 in Chinese.

Used as "Is Exactly"

Structure

就是 + Noun

Examples

- 那个人 就是 她的新男朋友。
  Nàge rén jiùshì tā de xīn nánpéngyou.
  That guy is her new boyfriend.
- 他 就是 你要找的人。
  Tā jiùshì nǐ yào zhǎo de rén.
  He's just the person that you're looking for.
- 我们 就是 他的家人。
  Wǒmen jiùshì tā de jiārén.
  We're his family.
- 你 就是 个笨蛋！
  Nǐ jiùshì gè bèndàn!
  A moron is precisely what you are!
- 他 就是 那个骗子！
  Tā jiùshì nàge piànzi!
  That con man is him!

Used as "Only Because"

就是 can be used to intensify the predicate to mean "only (because of) that and nothing else." In this case, 是 can't be omitted. In many cases, you could also add in an 因为, but it's not required.

Examples

- 他不去旅游 就是 不想花钱。
  Tā bù qù lǚyóu jiùshì bù xiǎng huāqián.
  He didn't travel only because he doesn't want to spend the money.
- 你不参加比赛 就是 怕输吗?
  Nǐ bù cānjiā bǐsài jiùshì pà shū ma?
  You're not entering the competition just because you're afraid of losing?
- 他这样说 就是 不喜欢我。
  Tā zhèyàng shuō jiùshì bù xǐhuan wǒ.
  He said this only because he doesn't like me.
- 她问这么多， 就是 担心你。
  She asked so many questions only because she's worried about you.
- 她 就是 漂亮，没别的优势。
  Tā jiùshì piàoliang, méi biéde yōushì.
  She's just pretty; she doesn't have any other strengths.

Other Usage

In the examples above, 就 pairs exclusively with the verb 是. But 就 can also come before other verbs, with similar emphatic effect. In these cases, it's also OK to use 就是 before the other verbs as well.

Structure

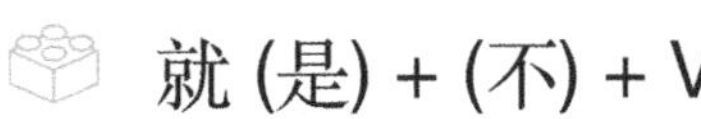

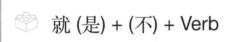

就 (是) + (不) + Verb

Examples

- 我 就 要去！
  Wǒ jiù yào qù!
  I just want to go!
- 我 就是 喜欢他。
  Wǒ jiù shì xǐhuan tā.
  I just like him.

- 我 就 不告诉你。
  Wǒ jiù bù gàosu nǐ.
  I'm just not going to tell you.
- 我父母 就是 不让我一个人去。
  Wǒ fùmǔ jiùshì bù ràng wǒ yīgèrén qù.
  My parents simply won't let me go alone.
- 这个学生 就是 不听老师的话。
  Zhège xuéshēng jiùshì bù tīng lǎoshī de huà.
  The student just wouldn't listen to his teacher.

As you may have noticed, many of these uses of 就 or 就是 carry a flippant, stubborn tone, referred to as 任性 (rènxìng) in Chinese.

Emphasizing quantity with "dou"

都 (dōu) is one of those words that on the surface may seem simple, but actually has many different subtle uses. In this article, we will look at using 都 (dōu) to emphasize quantity.

Structure

You can use 都 (dōu) to emphasize the large quantity of something. The subject should be some sort of large group (like a majority of people or things), e.g. 很多人 (hěn duō rén) or 大家 (dàjiā).

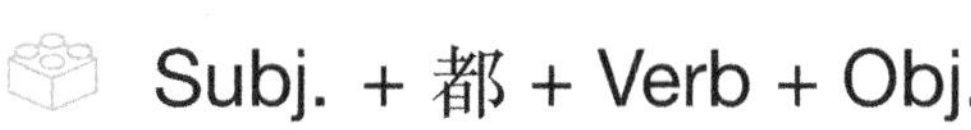

Subj. + 都 + Verb + Obj.

Examples with 很多 (hěn duō)

First let's look at some typical examples using 很多 (hěn duō) to emphasize that it's "a lot." Note that in English, it would be totally redundant and unnecessary to add "all" into these sentences, but in Chinese it's *totally natural* (and kind of weird not to). If you remember to follow the rule and keep using the 都 (dōu), eventually it will become more natural for you too.

- 很多 地方 都 有 wifi。
  Hěn duō dìfang dōu yǒu wifi.
  A lot of places have wifi.
- 我的 很多 朋友 都 有车。
  Wǒ de hěn duō péngyou dōu yǒu chē.
  A lot of my friends have cars.
- 很多 美国人 都 喜欢喝咖啡。
  Hěn duō Měiguó rén dōu xǐhuan hē kāfēi.
  A lot of Americans like drinking coffee.
- 很多 孩子 都 不喜欢上学。
  Hěn duō háizi dōu bù xǐhuan shàngxué.
  A lot of kids don't like to go to school.
- 很多 年轻人 都 想在大城市工作。
  Hěn duō niánqīng rén dōu xiǎng zài dà chéngshì gōngzuò.
  A lot of young people want to go to work in big cities.

Examples with 大家 (dàjiā)

Now let's look at some examples using 大家 (dàjiā) or "everyone." Again, in English, it would be totally redundant and unnecessary to add "all" into these sentences, but in Chinese it's *totally natural* (and kind of weird not to). You just have to get used to it.

- 大家 都 来了吗?
  Dàjiā dōu lái le ma?
  Is everyone here?
- 大家 都 应该知道。
  Dàjiā dōu yīnggāi zhīdào.
  Everyone should know.
- 大家 都 说你很聪明。
  Dàjiā dōu shuō nǐ hěn cōngming.
  Everyone says you're smart.
- 大家 都 忘了他的名字。
  Dàjiā dōu wàng le tā de míngzi.
  Everyone forgot his name.
- 大家 都 喜欢吃辣吗?
  Dàjiā dōu xǐhuan chī là ma?
  Does everyone like eating spicy food?

Examples with 每天 (měi tiān)

One other common way to use 都 (dōu) is when you're talking about something that happens really often, such as "every day": 每天 (měi tiān). Use 都 (dōu) here in Chinese, even if it feels unnatural. (Fake it 'til you make it!)

- 我 每天 都 要上班。
  Wǒ měi tiān dōu yào shàngbān.
  I have to go to work every day.
- 老师 每天 都 迟到。
  Lǎoshī měi tiān dōu chídào.
  The teacher comes late every day.
- 她 每天 都 不吃早饭。
  Tā měi tiān dōu bù chī zǎofàn.
  Every day, she does not eat breakfast.

- 我女朋友 每天 都 上淘宝。
  Wǒ nǚpéngyou měi tiān dōu shàng Táobǎo.
  My girlfriend goes on *Taobao* every day.
  Taobao is China's biggest online shopping website.
- 妈妈 每天 都 给我们做晚饭。
  Māma měi tiān dōu gěi wǒmen zuò wǎnfàn.
  Mom cooks dinner for us every day.

For more uses with 每 (měi), see also: Expressing "every" with "mei"[1].

Other Examples

Here are some other examples that don't use 很多 (hěn duō) or 大家 (dàjiā) or 每天 (měi tiān), but are still quite typical:

- 美国人 都 说英文。
  Měiguó rén dōu shuō Yīngwén.
  Americans all speak English.
- 我们五个人 都 去。
  Wǒmen wǔ gè rén dōu qù.
  All five of us are going.
- 四川人 都 喜欢吃辣。
  Sìchuān rén dōu xǐhuan chī là.
  Sichuanese people all like eating spicy food.
- 我的家人 都 没去过中国。
  Wǒ de jiārén dōu méi qù guo Zhōngguó.
  None of my family members has been to China.
- 我的学生 都 喜欢问问题。
  Wǒ de xuéshēng dōu xǐhuan wèn wèntí.
  My students all like to ask questions.

Similar to

- The "all" adverb "dou" (HSK1)
- Expressing "every time" with "mei" and "dou" (HSK2), page 203
- Expressing "all" with "suoyou" (HSK4)

1. Expressing "every" with "mei" (Grammar), page 158

Expressing "about to" with "jiuyao"

就要 (jiùyào) is similar to 快要 (kuàiyào), meaning "about to." They are interchangeable in some cases. But there is a major difference that you need to take a good look at.

Basic Pattern

Structure

(Subj. +) 就要 + Verb + 了 (, ……)

Examples

- 就要 下雨 了 。
  Jiù yào xiàyǔ le .
  It's about to rain.
- 他们 就要 结婚 了 。
  Tāmen jiù yào jiéhūn le .
  They are about to get married.
- 我 就要 出国 了 。
  Wǒ jiù yào chūguó le .
  I'm about to go abroad.
- 宝宝 就要 一岁 了 。
  Bǎobao jiù yào yī suì le .
  The baby is about to be one year old.
- 就要 下课 了 ，还有别的问题吗?
  Jiù yào xiàkè le , hái yǒu bié de wèntí ma?
  The class is almost over. Are there any other questions?

In this case, 就要 can be replaced by 快要 or 快[1].

---

1. Expressing "about to happen" with "le" (Grammar), page 188

Advanced Pattern

快要 (kuài yào) is generally "about to" [happen], but 就要 (jiù yào) could be used to mark a more specific time. 要 (yào) here can be omitted. For this one, you wouldn't normally use "about to" for this English translation, but the feeling is nevertheless that the impending event is coming up fast. This use of 就 (jiù) overlaps with its usage indicating earliness[1].

Structure

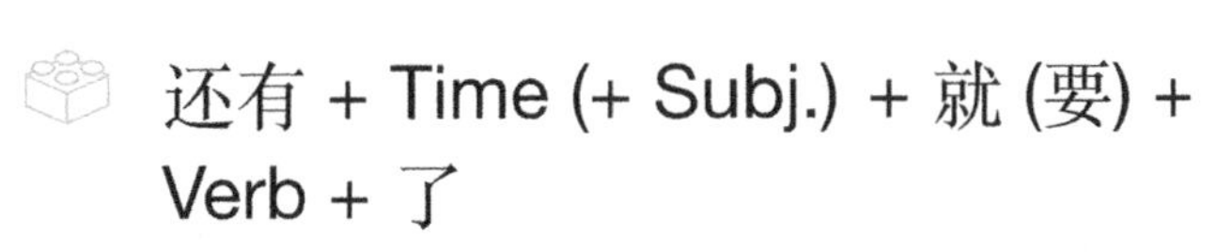
还有 + Time (+ Subj.) + 就 (要) + Verb + 了

Examples

- 还有十分钟我就下班了。
  Háiyǒu shí fēnzhōng wǒ jiù xiàbān le.
  I get off work in 10 minutes.
- 还有两个星期我们就要考试了。
  Háiyǒu liǎng gè xīngqí wǒmen jiù yào kǎoshì le.
  We're just two weeks away from the exam date.
- 还有一个月就要过年了。
  Háiyǒu yī gè yuè jiù yào guònián le.
  It will be Chinese New Year in another month.
- 还有半个小时飞机就起飞了。
  Háiyǒu bàn gè xiǎoshí fēijī jiù qǐfēi le.
  The plane takes off in half an hour.
- 还有五天就要放假了。
  Háiyǒu wǔ tiān jiù yào fàngjià le.
  I go on vacation in 5 days.

---

1. Expressing earliness with "jiu" (Grammar), page 31

Similar to

- Expressing "about to happen" with "le" (HSK2), page 188
- Expressing "be going to" with "yao" (HSK2), page 106
- Expressing "nearly" with "jihu" (HSK5)

Expressing "again" in the future with "zai"

While 又 (yòu) is used for "again" in the past, 再 (zài) is used for "again" in the future. That is, 再 is used when something has happened once and it *will* happen again.

Used as "Again"

Remember this is the *future* "again."

Structure

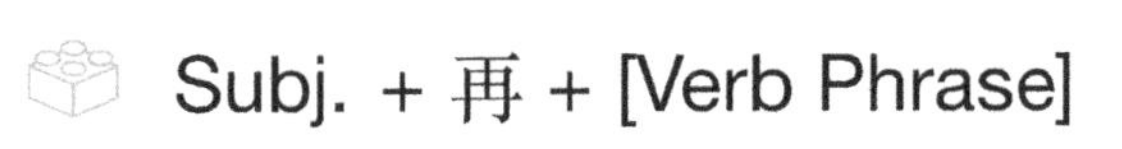

Subj. + 再 + [Verb Phrase]

Examples

- 我们明年 再 来。
  Wǒmen míngnián zài lái.
  We'll come again next year.
- 再 试一下。
  Zài shì yīxià.
  Try it again.
- 你可以 再 说一遍吗?
  Nǐ kěyǐ zài shuō yī biàn ma?
  Can you please say it again?
- 这本书我要 再 看一遍。
  Zhè běn shū wǒ yào zài kàn yī biàn.
  I want to read this book again.
- 你应该 再 复习一遍。
  Nǐ yīnggāi zài fùxí yī biàn.
  You should review it again.

In fact, this structure is present in one of the most common Chinese phrases: "再见!" In this case, it literally means "see you again."

Used as "Another" or "Some More"

The English word "another" is often avoided altogether by using 再.

Structure

Subj. + 再 + Verb + Obj.

In this case, the object includes a quantity phrase.

Examples

- 再 吃 一点 。
  Zài chī yīdiǎn .
  Eat some more.
- 再 点 几个菜 吧。
  Zài diǎn jǐ gè cài ba.
  Let's order some more dishes.
- 服务员, 再 来 两瓶啤酒 。
  Fúwùyuán, zài lái liǎng píng píjiǔ .
  Waiter, two more bottles of beer, please.
- 再 给我 三天时间 。
  Zài gěi wǒ sān tiān shíjiān .
  Give me another three days.
- 我能不能 再 拿 两个 ?
  Wǒ néng bu néng zài ná liǎng gè ?
  Can I take two more?

Used for Continuous Action

Here 再 is similar to the English "for a while longer" or "keep [going/doing]."

Structure

Examples

- 再 找找。
  Zài zhǎozhao.
  Keep looking.
- 你 再 问问。
  Nǐ zài wènwen.
  Keep asking.
- 别急，再 想想。
  Bié jí, zài xiǎngxiang.
  Don't worry. Keep thinking.

You can also add 一会儿 after the verb to mean "keep doing something a little longer."

- 再 聊一会儿。
  Zài liáo yīhuǐr.
  Keep talking for a little bit.
- 再 等一会儿。
  Zài děng yīhuǐr.
  Wait a little longer.

You can use either the "Verb + Verb" pattern or the 一会儿 pattern with 再, but don't use them together.

Similar to

- Comparing "zai" and "you" (HSK3)
- Expressing "again" in the past with "you" (HSK3)
- Sequencing with "xian" and "zai" (HSK3, HSK4)
- Expressing "the other" with "lingwai" (HSK4)
- Expressing "never again" with "zai ye bu" (HSK5)
- Expressing "over and over again" with "zaisan" (HSK5)

Expressing "already" with "dou"

都……了 (dōu... le) is a pattern used to express that something has already happened, similar to 已经 (yǐjīng)……了. However, 都……了 is used more emphatically, implying that the speaker holds some sort of attitude in relation to the event and is not merely objectively stating the facts, as with 已经……了. The two options can actually also be combined in the pattern 都已经……了. Here the meaning is the same as 都……了.

Used Before a Time

Structure

When 都……了 (dōu... le) is used at the beginning of a sentence, it will usually be followed with 还 (hái) or 还在 (hái zài). This implies that the other party should stop some kind of action.

都 + Time + 了

Examples

- 都九点了，快点起床！
  Dōu jiǔ diǎn le, kuài diǎn qǐchuáng!
  It's already nine o'clock. Get out of bed!
- 都十二点了，你还不睡？
  Dōu shí'èr diǎn le, nǐ hái bù shuì?
  It's already 12 o'clock. Aren't you going to bed?
- 都二十一世纪了，你还这么想？
  Dōu èrshí-yī shìjì le, nǐ hái zhème xiǎng?
  It's already the 21st century and you still think this way?
- 都一个小时了，他还在厕所里。
  Dōu yī gè xiǎoshí le, tā hái zài cèsuǒ lǐ.
  It's already been an hour, and he's still in the bathroom.
- 都一个星期了，还在下雨。
  Dōu yī gè xīngqī le, hái zài xiàyǔ.
  It's been a week and it's still raining.

Used Before the Predicate

Structure

Subj. + 都 + Predicate + 了

The predicate part of the pattern can be a verb or an adjective.

Examples

- 饭 都 凉 了 ，快吃吧。
  Fàn dōu liáng le , kuài chī ba.
  The food is cold already. Let's eat.
- 牛奶 都 坏 了 ，扔掉吧。
  Niúnǎi dōu huài le , rēngdiào ba.
  The milk's gone bad. Throw it out.
- 我 都 说了三遍 了 。别烦我！
  Wǒ dōu shuō le sān biàn le . Bié fán wǒ!
  I've said it three times already. Leave me alone!
- 这个电影你 都 看过 了 ，看别的吧。
  Zhège diànyǐng nǐ dōu kàn guo le , kàn biéde ba.
  You've seen this movie already. Let's watch something else.
- 他 都 道歉 了 ，你别生气了。
  Tā dōu dàoqiàn le , nǐ bié shēngqì le.
  He already apologized. Stop being so mad at him.

Similar to

- Expressing “already” with “yijing” (HSK2), page 22
- Expressing “already” with just “le” (HSK2), page 75
- Expressing duration of inaction (HSK3)

Expressing "already" with "yijing"

已经⋯⋯了 (yǐjīng... le) is the basic pattern used to express "already" in Chinese. It's easy to forget the 了 (le) on the end, but using it will make your Chinese more natural.

Basic Usages

已经 (yǐjīng) with Verb Phrases

Structure

The most common structure is to use 已经⋯⋯了 (yǐjīng... le) with a verb phrase.

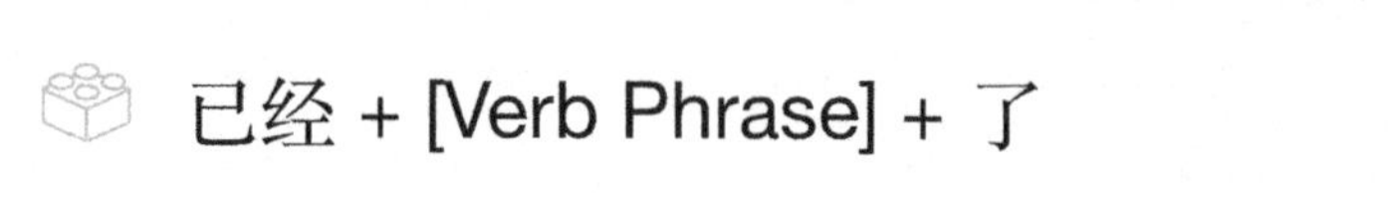

Examples

- 他们 已经 走 了 。 *with just a verb*
  Tāmen yǐjīng zǒu le.
  They've already left.
- 我 已经 有男朋友 了 。 *with a verb phrase*
  Wǒ yǐjīng yǒu nánpéngyou le.
  I already have a boyfriend.
- 宝宝 已经 会说话 了 。 *with a verb phrase*
  Bǎobao yǐjīng huì shuōhuà le.
  The baby can already speak.
- 妈妈 已经 回来 了 。 *with just a verb*
  Māma yǐjīng huílái le.
  Mom has already come back.
- 他 已经 上飞机 了 。 *with a verb phrase*
  Tā yǐjīng shàng fēijī le.
  He's already gotten on the plane.

已经 (yǐjīng) with Adjectives

Structure

Sometimes an adjective or a time noun is used instead of a typical verb phrase:

已经 + (很 +) Adj. + 了

Examples

- 爸爸妈妈 已经 老 了 。
  Bàba māma yǐjīng lǎo le.
  Mom and dad are already old.
- 已经 很便宜 了 。
  Yǐjīng hěn piányi le.
  It is already very cheap.
- 你女朋友 已经 很漂亮 了 ！
  Nǐ nǚpéngyou yǐjīng hěn piàoliang le!
  Your girlfriend is already very beautiful!
- 你的感冒 已经 好 了 吗?
  Nǐ de gǎnmào yǐjīng hǎo le ma?
  Is your cold already better?
- 已经 很晚 了 ，我们走吧。
  Yǐjīng hěn wǎn le, wǒmen zǒu ba.
  It's already really late. Let's go.

已经 (yǐjīng) with Time Nouns

A "time noun" simply refers to almost any word in Chinese indicating a time something happened.

Structure

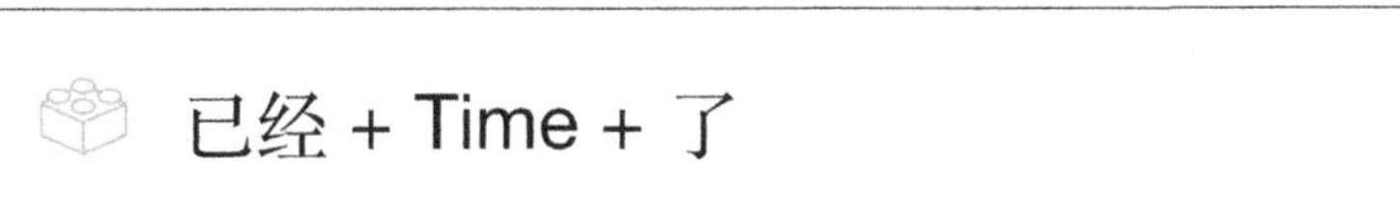

Examples

- 已经 11 点 了 ，女儿还没回来。
  Yǐjīng shíyī diǎn le, nǚ'ér hái méi huílái.
  It is already 11 o'clock, and my daughter has not returned.
- 爷爷 已经 八十五岁 了 。
  Yéye yǐjīng bāshí-wǔ suì le.
  Grandpa is already eighty-five years old.
- 我学习中文 已经 一年 了 。
  Wǒ xuéxí Zhōngwén yǐjīng yī nián le.
  I have already been studying Chinese for a year.
- 他在洗手间里 已经 半个小时 了 。
  Tā zài xǐshǒujiān lǐ yǐjīng bàn gè xiǎoshí le.
  He has already been in the bathroom for half an hour.
- 爸爸去北京出差 已经 两天 了 。
  Bàba qù Běijīng chūchāi yǐjīng liǎng tiān le.
  It has already been two days since dad went to Beijing on business trip.

Negative Form

Structure

The negative structure simply adds a 不 (bù) after 已经 (yǐjīng), and before the verb (or possibly adjective).

已经 + 不 + Verb + 了

Examples

Generally this negative 已经 (yǐjīng) structure is translated into English as "not… anymore" rather than using the word "already."

- 我 已经 不 喜欢你 了 。
  Wǒ yǐjīng bù xǐhuan nǐ le.
  I don't like you anymore.

- 他 已经 不 爱他的猫 了 。
  Tā yǐjīng bù ài tā de māo le.
  He doesn't love his cat anymore.
- 他们 已经 不 住在中国 了 。
  Tāmen yǐjīng bù zhù zài Zhōngguó le.
  They don't live in China anymore.
- 我 已经 不 需要父母的钱 了 。
  Wǒ yǐjīng bù xūyào fùmǔ de qián le.
  I don't need my parents' money anymore.
- 你 已经 不 在 Google 工作 了 吗?
  Nǐ yǐjīng bù zài Google gōngzuò le ma?
  You don't work at Google anymore?

Similar to

- Expressing "already" with "dou" (HSK2), page 20
- Expressing "already" with just "le" (HSK2), page 75

Expressing "and also" with "hai"

In English we use "and also" when we want to connect separate and different thoughts. We can do the same thing in Chinese by using 还 (hái).

Structure

The adverb 还 (hái) can be used to link two phrases together, in a similar way to "and also" in English. In this case, 还 (hái) begins a new phrase or clause.

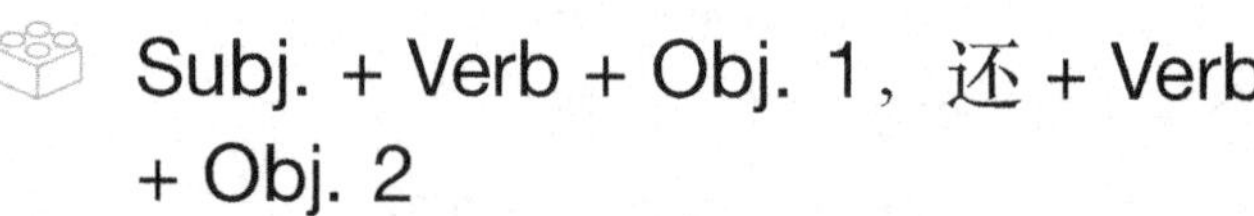

Examples

- 她有一个弟弟，还 有一个妹妹。
  Tā yǒu yī gè dìdi, hái yǒu yī gè mèimei.
  She has a younger brother and also has a younger sister.
- 我老板会说法语，还 会说日语。
  Wǒ lǎobǎn huì shuō Fǎyǔ, hái huì shuō Rìyǔ.
  My boss can speak French and can also speak Japanese.
- 你要一杯咖啡，还 要什么？
  Nǐ yào yī bēi kāfēi, hái yào shénme?
  You want a cup of coffee, and what else do you want?
- 我想吃冰淇淋，还 想吃汉堡。
  Wǒ xiǎng chī bīngqílín, hái xiǎng chī hànbǎo.
  I want to eat ice cream and I also want to eat a hamburger.
- 爸爸有一个小米手机，还 有一个 iPhone。
  Bàba yǒu yī gè Xiǎomǐ shǒujī, hái yǒu yī gè iPhone.
  Dad has a Xiaomi phone and also has an iPhone.
- 你晚上在家做了作业，还 做了什么？
  Nǐ wǎnshang zài jiā zuò le zuòyè, hái zuò le shénme?
  You did your homework at home tonight, and what else did you do?

- 他结婚的时候，请了同事，还 请了谁？

  Tā jiéhūn de shíhou, qǐng le tóngshì, hái qǐng le shéi?

  When he got married, he invited his co-workers. Who else did he invite?

- 生日的时候，我们会吃蛋糕，还 要送礼物。

  Shēngrì de shíhou, wǒmen huì chī dàngāo, hái yào sòng lǐwù.

  During a birthday, we eat cake and also give presents.

- 去美国要带钱、护照，还 要带什么？

  Qù Měiguó yào dài qián, hùzhào, hái yào dài shénme?

  To go to the USA, you need to take money and a passport. What else do you need to take with you?

The Difference Between 还 (hái) and 也 (yě)

It should be noted that another common way to express "also" is with the word 也 (yě). What's the difference? With 还 (hái), ONE subject is doing TWO different things, whereas when 也 (yě) is used, TWO subjects are doing ONE thing.

It's the difference between these two English sentences:

- He fixed dinner **and also** washed the dishes.
- She washed the dishes **too**.

If you translated these into Chinese, the first one (one subject, two actions) would use 还 (hái), and the second one (second subject, no new actions) would use 也 (yě). Let's do that!

- 他做了饭，还 洗了碗。

  Tā zuò le fàn, hái xǐ le wǎn.

  He fixed dinner and also washed the dishes.

- 她 也 洗了碗。

  Tā yě xǐ le wǎn.

  She washed the dishes too.

How about a few more similar examples?

- 我洗了澡，还 洗了衣服。

  Wǒ xǐ le zǎo, hái xǐ le yīfu.

  I took a shower and also did my laundry.

- 她 也 洗了衣服。

  Tā yě xǐ le yīfu.

  She did her laundry too.

- 我们今天晚上出去吃饭了，还 看了电影。
  Wǒmen jīntiān wǎnshang chūqù chīfàn le, hái kàn le diànyǐng.
  We went out for dinner tonight and also watched a movie.
- 他们今天晚上 也 看了电影。
  Tāmen jīntiān wǎnshang yě kàn le diànyǐng.
  They watched a movie tonight too.

Similar to

- The "also" adverb "ye" (HSK1)
- Continuation with "hai" (HSK2), page 5
- Moderating positive adjectives with "hai" (HSK2), page 48
- Expressing "except" and "in addition" with "chule· · · yiwai" (HSK3)
- Expressing "not only… but also" (HSK3)
- Expressing "in addition" with "haiyou" (HSK4)
- Advanced uses of "hai" (HSK5)

Expressing "then" with "jiu"

The adverb 就 (jiù) has quite a few uses in Chinese, and appears in several common patterns. This is the first and simplest usage you need to know, though, and it means something similar to "then."

Structure

Usually the first part of the sentence will set up a situation. Then the second part, with 就 (jiù) leading the way, indicates what should be done as a result.

 ..., 就 + Verb Phrase

Examples

Not always easy to translate, you could think of 就 (jiù) as meaning "just" or "then."

- 你喜欢喝奶茶，我们 就 买奶茶吧。
  Nǐ xǐhuan hē nǎichá, wǒmen jiù mǎi nǎichá ba.
  So you like milk tea. Then we'll buy milk tea.
- 你最有经验， 就 听你的吧。
  Nǐ zuì yǒu jīngyàn, jiù tīng nǐ de ba.
  You have the most experience. We'll just listen to you.
- 我听到这个坏消息， 就 给你打电话了。
  Wǒ tīngdào zhège huài xiāoxi, jiù gěi nǐ dǎ diànhuà le.
  As soon as I heard this bad news, I called you.
- 你现在身体不好， 就 不要喝酒了。
  Nǐ xiànzài shēntǐ bù hǎo, jiù bù yào hē jiǔ le..
  Your health isn't good now. So just stop drinking.
- 他最近太累了， 就 生病了。
  Tā zuìjìn tài lèi le, jiù shēngbìng le.
  He's been too tired recently, and then he got sick.

- 今天下雨，我们 就 不出去了。
  Jīntiān xiàyǔ, wǒmen jiù bù chūqù le.
  It's going to rain today. So let's just not go out.
- 他妈妈没有给他买书包，他 就 哭了。
  Tā māma méiyǒu gěi tā mǎi shūbāo, tā jiù kū le.
  His mom didn't buy him the backpack, and then he just started crying.
- 就 在这家店吃饭吧，那家店人太多了。
  Jiù zài zhè jiā diàn chīfàn ba, nà jiā diàn rén tài duō le .
  Let's just eat at this restaurant. That one is too crowded.
- 就 去看电影吧。
  Jiù qù kàn diànyǐng ba.
  Let's just go watch a movie.

Similar to

- Expressing earliness with "jiu" (HSK2), page 31
- Expressing "as one likes" with "jiu" (HSK3)
- Expressing "if" with "ruguo… dehua" (HSK3)
- Expressing "if… then…" with "ruguo… jiu…" (HSK3)

Expressing earliness with "jiu"

Just as 才 (cái) can express lateness, 就 (jiù) can be used to indicate that something happened earlier or sooner than expected. It can also be used in the near future to indicate something will happen very soon.

Used as "Right Away" (in the Future)

When something happens "right away," you're talking about "very soon" in the *future*.

Structure

The pattern is as follows:

Examples

- 我马上 就 来。
  Wǒ mǎshàng jiù lái.
  I'll be there in a second.
- 米饭二十分钟 就 好。
  Mǐfàn èrshí fēnzhōng jiù hǎo.
  The rice will be ready in 20 minutes.
- 你们现在 就 出门吗?
  Nǐmen xiànzài jiù chūmén ma?
  Are you leaving the house right now?
- 他们一会儿 就 到。
  Tāmen yīhuìr jiù dào.
  They will be here in a few minutes.
- 老板明天 就 回来。
  Lǎobǎn míngtiān jiù huílái.
  The boss will be back tomorrow.

Note that it can sometimes be hard to translate the feeling of "soonness" into English, but in every one of these examples, the time given in the sentences *feels "soon"* to the speaker.

Used as "Early" (in the Past)

Structure

This use of 就 might be translated "as early as," but usually the earliness is not specifically marked in English.

> Subj. + [Point in Time] + 就 + Verb + 了

Examples

- 我们九点上课，他八点 就 来 了 。
  Wǒmen jiǔ diǎn shàngkè, tā bā diǎn jiù lái le .
  We have class at nine, but he came in at eight.
- 飞机十点起飞，他六点 就 到机场 了 。
  Fēijī shí diǎn qǐfēi, tā liù diǎn jiù dào jīchǎng le .
  The plane takes off at ten o'clock, but he arrived at the airport at six.
- 我昨晚八点半 就 睡觉 了 。
  Wǒ zuówǎn bā diǎn bàn jiù shuìjiào le .
  I went to bed at eight thirty last night.
- 她十八岁 就 大学毕业 了 。
  Tā shíbā suì jiù dàxué bìyè le .
  She graduated from college when she was only 18 years old.

Not only can 就 emphasize a "point in time," but it can also emphasize a "time period," indicating that something happened very quickly.

> Subj. + Time Period + 就 + Verb + 了

A few examples:

- 你 一个晚上 就 看完 了 ?
  Nǐ yī gè wǎnshang jiù kàn wán le ?
  It only took you just one night to finish reading it?
- 他 十分钟 就 做完 了 。
  Tā shí fēnzhōng jiù zuò wán le .
  It only took him ten minutes to finish doing it.

From the example sentences it is clear that 了 naturally occurs with a verb used after 就. This is because verbs following 就 generally have the feeling of being completed.

Colloquial Saying 早就

早就 means "long ago," and is usually used to express a kind of impatience or surprise on the part of the speaker. It comes before the verb.

- 我 早就 知道 了 !
  Wǒ zǎo jiù zhīdào le !
  I knew that long ago!
- 她 早就 结婚 了 。
  Tā zǎo jiù jiéhūn le .
  She got married a long time ago.
- 他们 早就 分手 了 。
  Tāmen zǎo jiù fēnshǒu le .
  They broke up a long time ago.
- 我们 早就 毕业 了 。
  Wǒmen zǎo jiù bìyè le .
  We graduated a long time ago!
- 我 早就 跟你说 过 , 他不是好人。
  Wǒ zǎo jiù gēn nǐ shuō guo , tā bù shì hǎo rén.
  I told you a long time ago that he's not a good guy.

Similar to

- Expressing "then" with "jiu" (HSK2), page 29
- Comparing "cai" and "jiu" (HSK3)
- Expressing lateness with "cai" (HSK3)
- Events in quick succession with "yi… jiu…" (HSK4)

Negative commands with "bie"

Instead of saying "do not" with 不要 (bùyào)[1], we can say "don't" a little more quickly and forcefully by using 别 (bié).

Structure

Besides using 不要 (bùyào)[1], negative commands can also be formed with 别 (bié). You could think of 别 (bié) as a contraction of 不要 (bùyào), as the structure is the same for both:

 别 + Verb (+ Obj.)

Examples

- 别 走。
  Bié zǒu.
  Don't leave.
- 别 说话！
  Bié shuōhuà!
  Don't speak!
- 别 笑！
  Bié xiào!
  Don't laugh!
- 别 动！
  Bié dòng!
  Don't move!
- 别 过来！
  Bié guòlái!
  Don't come over here!
- 别 打孩子！
  Bié dǎ háizi!
  Don't hit the child!

---

1. Negative commands with "buyao" (Grammar), page 118

- 别 喝太多。
  Bié hē tài duō.
  Don't drink too much.
- 喝酒以后 别 开车。
  Hējiǔ yǐhòu bié kāichē.
  After drinking alcohol, don't drive.
- 吃饭的时候 别 玩手机。
  Chīfàn de shíhou bié wán shǒujī.
  When eating, don't play with your cell phone.
- 上课的时候 别 说英文。
  Shàngkè de shíhou bié shuō Yīngwén.
  Don't speak English in class.

Similar to

- Expressing “stop doing” with “bie· · · le” (HSK2), page 194
- Negative commands with “buyao” (HSK2), page 118
- Expressing “don’t need to” with “buyong” (HSK4)

Asking about degree with "duo"

How big? How busy? How cold? Ask questions like these regarding the degree of an adjective with 多 (duō). This is just one of the many uses of this word.

Structure

多 (duō) is often used to ask about the degree or extent of something.

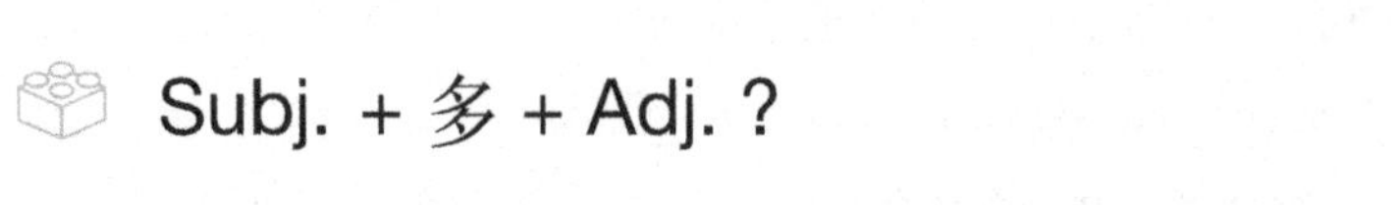

This is an easy way to ask "How [adjective] is [subject]?"

Examples

- 她 多 高?
  Tā duō gāo?
  How tall is she?
- 你家 多 大?
  Nǐ jiā duō dà?
  How large is your house?
- 你的孩子 多 大?
  Nǐ de háizi duō dà?
  How old is your child?
- 黄河 多 长?
  Huánghé duō cháng?
  How long is the Yellow River?
- 你家离这儿 多 远?
  Nǐ jiā lí zhèr duō yuǎn?
  How far is your house away from here?
- 你要在美国待 多 久?
  Nǐ yào zài Měiguó dāi duō jiǔ?
  How long are you going to stay in the USA?

- 这些东西 多 重?
  Zhèxiē dōngxi duō zhòng?
  How heavy are these things?
- 你知道我们现在 多 胖吗?
  Nǐ zhīdào wǒmen xiànzài duō pàng ma?
  Do you know how fat we are now?
- 你知道这里的冬天 多 冷吗?
  Nǐ zhīdào zhèlǐ de dōngtiān duō lěng ma?
  Do you know how cold it is here in winter?
- 你知道上海的房子 多 贵吗?
  Nǐ zhīdào Shànghǎi de fángzi duō guì ma?
  Do you know how expensive housing is in Shanghai?

大 (dà) and 小 (xiǎo) can also be used to describe ages. The question phrase 多大 (duō dà) is often used to ask "how old." However, it is an informal way to ask, usually reserved for peers, close friends, or children. The phrase 几岁 (jǐ suì) is most often used for children young enough to display their ages on one hand. Adults do not normally directly ask each other's ages in a formal setting.

Similar to

- Indicating a number in excess (HSK2), page 63
- Intensifying with "duo" (HSK3)
- Doing something more with "duo" (HSK4)

Expressing "a little too" with "you dian"

At times you may want to politely diss something using the phrase "a little too." For example, if you are getting lunch with a friend who wants to be seated outside, you might say, "It is a little too hot" to suggest you sit inside. In a case like this, you can use 有一点 (yǒuyīdiǎn) or 有点 (yǒudiǎn). The two are interchangeable.

Structure

To say that something is "a little *too*..." or "a bit *too*...," 有一点 (yǒuyīdiǎn) is often used. Its northern Chinese version is 有一点儿 (yǒuyīdiǎnr).

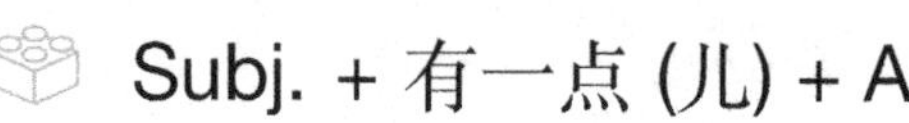

In spoken Chinese, the 一 (yī) in 有一点 (yǒuyīdiǎn) is often dropped, leaving 有点 (yǒudiǎn). In northern China, that's usually pronounced 有点儿 (yǒudiǎnr).

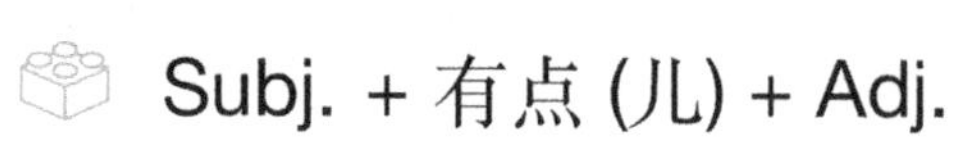

Examples

- 我有点饿。
  Wǒ yǒudiǎn è.
  I'm a little hungry.
- 这个菜有点辣。
  Zhège cài yǒudiǎn là.
  This dish is a little too spicy.
- 昨天有一点热。
  Zuótiān yǒuyīdiǎn rè.
  Yesterday it was a little too hot.
- 上海的冬天有一点冷。
  Shànghǎi de dōngtiān yǒuyīdiǎn lěng.
  Winter in Shanghai is a bit too cold.

- 我弟弟 有点 胖。
  Wǒ dìdi yǒudiǎn pàng.
  My younger brother is a bit fat.
- 今天 有点 累。
  Jīntiān yǒudiǎn lèi.
  Today I am a little bit tired.
- 这个月公司 有点 忙。
  Zhège yuè gōngsī yǒudiǎn máng.
  This month the company is a little bit busy.
- 这个地方 有点 吵，我们走吧。
  Zhège dìfang yǒudiǎn chǎo, wǒmen zǒu ba.
  This place is a little too noisy. Let's go.
- 爸爸回来 有点 晚，妈妈 有点 不高兴。
  Bàba huílái yǒudiǎn wǎn, māma yǒudiǎn bù gāoxìng.
  Dad came back home a bit too late, so mom was a little unhappy.
- 老师今天 有点 不舒服，所以没来上课。
  Lǎoshī jīntiān yǒudiǎn bù shūfu, suǒyǐ méi lái shàngkè.
  Today, the teacher felt a little unwell, so she didn't come to class.

Negative Connotation

Note that for the speaker, the adjective after 有点 (yǒudiǎn) expresses an unpleasant or undesirable meaning, so you won't hear things like 有点高兴 (yǒudiǎn gāoxìng), 有点舒服 (yǒudiǎn shūfu), 有点好玩儿 (yǒudiǎn hǎowánr), etc., because "happy," "comfortable," and "fun" are all adjectives with positive connotations.

Similar to

- Simple "noun + adjective" sentences (HSK1)
- Expressing "much more" in comparisons (HSK2, HSK3), page 205
- Comparing "youdian" and "yidian" (HSK3)
- Expressing "even more" with "geng" or "hai" (HSK3)
- Expressing "rather" with "bijiao" (HSK3)
- Using "youde" to mean "some" (HSK3)
- Expressing "quite" with "ting" (HSK4)

Expressing "even more" with "geng"

To express "even more," (as in "even more expensive," "even more ridiculous," "even more badass"), you can use 更 (gèng). 更 (gèng) generally comes before adjectives.

Basic Usage

Structure

The pattern in Chinese is simple:

Note that this pattern is not simply a way of adding "-er" to an adjective or a substitute for 比 (bǐ) comparisons[1]. In each case, you're adding "even more" to an existing considerable amount, as in, "I'm already rich, but I want to be even richer."

Examples

- 这两个银行哪个 更 近?
  Zhè liǎng gè yínháng nǎge gèng jìn?
  Between these two banks, which one is closer?
- 我想找一个 更 帅的男朋友。
  Wǒ xiǎng zhǎo yī gè gèng shuài de nánpéngyou.
  I want to find a more handsome boyfriend.
  It is implied that my boyfriend now is already handsome, but I want to find an even more handsome boyfriend.
- 我喜欢在网上买书，因为 更 便宜。
  Wǒ xǐhuan zài wǎngshàng mǎi shū, yīnwèi gèng piányi.
  I like buying books online because it's cheaper.
- 不要太高兴，我们还有 更 多的工作要做。
  Bùyào tài gāoxìng, wǒmen hái yǒu gèng duō de gōngzuò yào zuò.
  Don't get too excited. We still have more work to do.
  It is implied that a lot of work has already been done but there is still "even more" work left.

1. Basic comparisons with "bi" (Grammar), page 86

- 结婚以后，她变得 更 漂亮了。

  Jiéhūn yǐhòu, tā biàn de gèng piàoliang le.

  She's become more beautiful after she got married.

Structure with 比 (bǐ)

While 更 (gèng) is not a substitute for 比 (bǐ) (the classic comparison word)[1], the two can be used together.

Structure

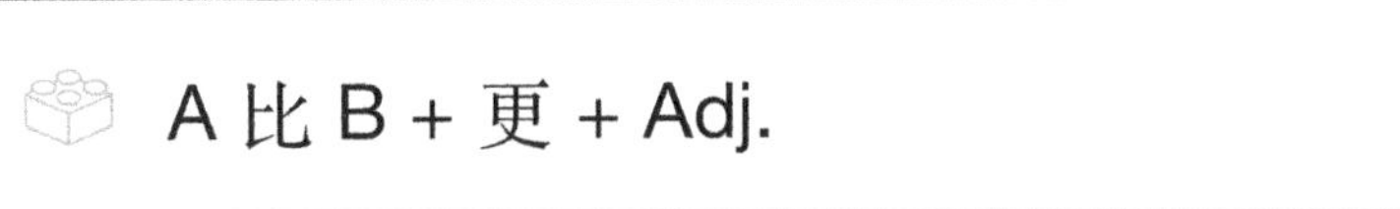

This expresses that "A is **even more** Adj. than B."

Examples

- 北京的房子 比 上海 更 贵。

  Běijīng de fángzi bǐ Shànghǎi gèng guì.

  The houses in Beijing are even more expensive than those in Shanghai.

- 春节 比 中秋节 更 热闹。

  Chūnjié bǐ Zhōngqiūjié gèng rènao.

  Spring Festival is even more boisterous than Mid-autumn Festival.

- 汉字 比 声调 更 难。

  Hànzì bǐ shēngdiào gèng nán.

  Chinese characters are even more difficult than tones.

- 他现在的女朋友 比 以前的 更 漂亮。

  Tā xiànzài de nǚpéngyou bǐ yǐqián de gèng piàoliang.

  His current girlfriend is even more beautiful than his previous one.

- 中国的高铁 比 飞机 更 方便。

  Zhōngguó de gāotiě bǐ fēijī gèng fāngbiàn.

  China's high-speed trains are even more convenient than airplanes.

---

1. Basic comparisons with "bi" (Grammar), page 86

Similar to

- Basic comparisons with “bi” (HSK2), page 86
- Superlative “zui” (HSK2), page 53

Expressing "really" with "zhen"

As an adverb, the word 真 (zhēn) means "really" or "truly."

真 (zhēn) Before an Adjective

Structure

真 (zhēn) is used only in exclamatory sentences and comes before an adjective.

真 + Adj.

Example

- 你 真 好！
  Nǐ zhēn hǎo!
  You are so nice!
- 你女朋友 真 漂亮！
  Nǐ nǚpéngyou zhēn piàoliang!
  Your girlfriend is really pretty!
- 他家 真 有钱！
  Tā jiā zhēn yǒuqián!
  His family is really rich!
- 小狗 真 可爱！
  Xiǎogǒu zhēn kě'ài!
  This puppy is really cute!
- 今天 真 热！
  Jīntiān zhēn rè!
  It's truly hot today!

真 (zhēn) Before Certain Verbs or 能 (néng) / 会 (huì)

We don't want to get too technical on you, but there are certain other words that can be jazzed up with 真 (zhēn). One type of word is auxiliary verbs, like 能 (néng) and 会 (huì). The other type is psychological verbs like 喜欢 (xǐhuan).

Structure

 真 + Verb

Example

- 你妈妈 真 爱你！
  Nǐ māma zhēn ài nǐ!
  Your mother really loves you!
- 我 真 喜欢住在中国！
  Wǒ zhēn xǐhuan zhù zài Zhōngguó!
  I really like living in China!
- 我 真 讨厌这种男人！
  Wǒ zhēn tǎoyàn zhè zhǒng nánrén!
  I really hate this kind of guy!
- 你 真 会说话！
  Nǐ zhēn huì shuōhuà!
  You are so good with words!
- 你 真 能吃！
  Nǐ zhēn néng chī!
  You ate so much!

Similar to

- Superlative “zui” (HSK2), page 53
- Intensifying with “duo” (HSK3)
- Expressing “quite” with “ting” (HSK4)

Expressing distance with "li"

Are we there yet? One of the ways to express distance is to use 离 (lí). The word order might seem a little tricky at first, but once you get it down, you'll be able to talk about distance with no problem.

Using 离 (lí) in a Statement

Structure

Unless you're talking about a very specific distance, you'll normally want to pair 离 (lí) with the adjective 近 (jìn) for "close," or 远 (yuǎn) for "far."

Place 1 + 离 + Place 2 + Adv. + 近 / 远

So this pattern is normally used to simply express that one place is (not) close or (not) far from another place. Easy, right? It's learning the sentence pattern that usually trips learners up, because it doesn't feel like natural word order to a speaker of English.

Examples

- 我家 离 公司很近。
  Wǒ jiā lí gōngsī hěn jìn.
  My house is close to my office.
- 美国 离 中国很远。
  Měiguó lí Zhōngguó hěn yuǎn.
  The USA is far from China.
- 这个酒店 离 火车站很近。
  Zhège jiǔdiàn lí huǒchēzhàn hěn jìn.
  This hotel is very close to the train station.
- 那个酒吧 离 这儿太远了，我不想去。
  Nàge jiǔbā lí zhèr tài yuǎn le, wǒ bù xiǎng qù.
  That bar is too far away from here. I don't want to go.
- 我不想去 离 家很远的地方工作。
  Wǒ bù xiǎng qù lí jiā hěn yuǎn de dìfang gōngzuò.
  I don't want to go work at a place very far away from home.

Using 离 (lí) in a Question

Structure

These two sentence patterns are extremely common in everyday conversations when discussing distances.

> Place 1 + 离 + Place 2 (+ Adv.) + 近 / 远 + 吗?

> Place 1 + 离 + Place 2 (+ 有) + 多远?

Note that in English, you can actually ask, "How close is it from here?" if the distance is obviously short. But in Chinese it's just, "How far is it from here?"

Examples

- 你家 离 超市远吗?
  Nǐ jiā lí chāoshì yuǎn ma?
  Is your house far away from the supermarket?
- 你的大学 离 你老家很远吗?
  Nǐ de dàxué lí nǐ lǎojiā hěn yuǎn ma?
  Is your college very far away from your hometown?
- 你们公司 离 地铁站近吗?
  Nǐmen gōngsī lí dìtiězhàn jìn ma?
  Is your company close to the metro station?
- 你家 离 学校多远?
  Nǐ jiā lí xuéxiào duō yuǎn?
  How far is it from your home to school?
- 这个酒店 离 机场有多远?
  Zhège jiǔdiàn lí jīchǎng yǒu duō yuǎn?
  How far is it from this hotel to the airport?

Expressing “Stay Away from Me” with 离 (lí)

One final example is a command, commonly heard in colloquial Chinese:

- 你 离 我远点儿！
  Nǐ lí wǒ yuǎn diǎnr!
  Stay away from me.

It’s a somewhat atypical usage when compared with the others, because it uses two people rather than two places. The sentence literally means, “Distance yourself from me further.” In other words, “Stay away from me,” or “Don’t come near me.”

Similar to

- Expressing “from· · · to· · ·” with “cong· · · dao· · ·” (HSK2), page 92
- Comparing “li” and “cong” (HSK4)

Moderating positive adjectives with "hai"

Whenever you want to imply that something is "good," but also kind of "meh," you can use 还 (hái) in front of the "good" adjective.

Commonly Used Expressions

Besides expressing continuation[1], 还 (hái) can also be used to weaken positive adjectives. Used with the adjective "good," this is similar to saying "fairly good" or "pretty good" in English. It's also sometimes used by a speaker to be more modest. Below are some of the most common adjectives that get "toned down" by 还 (hái) in this structure.

Structure

 Subj. + 还 + 好 / 可以 / 行 / 不错

In this pattern, 好 (hǎo), 可以 (kěyǐ), 行 (xíng), and 不错 (bùcuò) combined with 还 ()hái can all be taken to mean "pretty good" or "all right" or "decent" (but also kind of *meh*... not *great*). As in English, intonation and facial expressions help convey the meaning. If expectations were already low to begin with, 还可以 (hái kěyǐ) can have the sense of "pretty darn good;" it all depends on context and tone of voice.

Examples

- 我 还好 。
  Wǒ hái hǎo.
  I'm OK.
- 爸爸做的菜 还可以 。
  Bàba zuò de cài hái kěyǐ.
  The food that dad cooks is OK.
- 我们老板 还不错 。
  Wǒmen lǎobǎn hái bùcuò.
  Our boss is not too bad.

---

1. Continuation with "hai" (Grammar), page 5

- 这家店 还行 ，不太贵。
  Zhè jià diàn hái xíng , bù tài guì.
  This shop is OK. It's not too expensive.
- 我男朋友的工资 还可以 。
  Wǒ nánpéngyou de gōngzī hái kěyǐ .
  My boyfriend's salary is OK.
- 新的办公室 还不错 。
  Xīn de bàngōngshì hái bùcuò .
  The new office is OK.
- 我觉得这里的菜 还可以 ，没有那么难吃。
  Wǒ juéde zhèlǐ de cài hái kěyǐ , méiyǒu nàme nánchī.
  I think the food here is OK, it is not too bad-tasting.
- 这个牌子 还不错 ，很多年轻人喜欢。
  Zhège páizi hái bùcuò ，hěn duō niánqīng rén xǐhuan.
  This brand is not too bad. Many young people like it.
- 房子 还可以 ，但是有点贵。
  Fángzi hái kěyǐ , dànshì yǒudiǎn guì.
  The apartment is not too bad, but it is a bit expensive.

Similar to

- Continuation with “hai” (HSK2), page 5
- Expressing “and also” with “hai” (HSK2), page 26
- Superlative “zui” (HSK2), page 53
- Advanced uses of “hai” (HSK5)

Modifying nouns with phrase + “de”

In addition to linking adjectives to nouns, 的 (de) can also be used to link a whole phrase to a noun, making the already useful 的 (de) even more useful.

With a Noun

As well as attaching adjectives to nouns, 的 (de) can be used to attach whole phrases to nouns. In English this is often achieved with “who” or “that.” For example, “the man who went to Beijing” or “the book that I bought yesterday.”

Structure

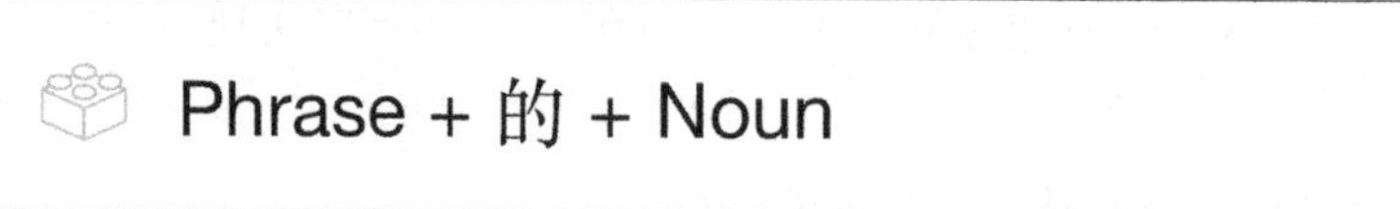

Here the phrase is typically of the form “Noun + Verb.” The pattern, by itself, doesn’t make clear whether the action happened in the past, present, or future.

Examples

- 妈妈做 的 菜
  māma zuò de cài
  the food that mom cooks / cooked
- 去北京 的 火车
  qù Běijīng de huǒchē
  the train that goes / went to Beijing
- 你教 的 学生
  nǐ jiāo de xuésheng
  the students that you teach / taught
- 老板请 的 朋友
  lǎobǎn qǐng de péngyou
  the friends that the boss invites / invited
- 我画 的 画
  wǒ huà de huà
  the pictures that I draw / drew

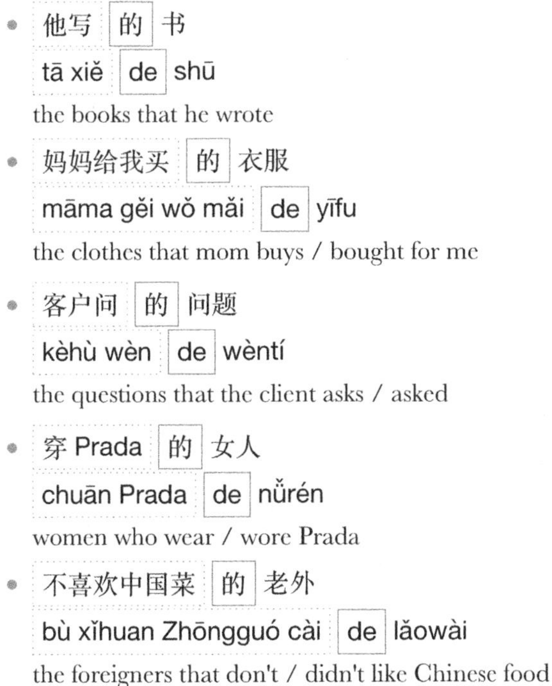

- 他写 的 书
  tā xiě de shū
  the books that he wrote
- 妈妈给我买 的 衣服
  māma gěi wǒ mǎi de yīfu
  the clothes that mom buys / bought for me
- 客户问 的 问题
  kèhù wèn de wèntí
  the questions that the client asks / asked
- 穿 Prada 的 女人
  chuān Prada de nǚrén
  women who wear / wore Prada
- 不喜欢中国菜 的 老外
  bù xǐhuan Zhōngguó cài de lǎowài
  the foreigners that don't / didn't like Chinese food

Without a Noun

In some cases, it is possible to drop the noun from the pattern, and just use the "Noun + 的 (de)." This is kind of like saying "what Mom made" or "the red one" in English. In Chinese the 的 (de) serves the same purpose as the English word "what." By using this pattern, you can avoid repeating the same noun over and over again unnecessarily. Just be sure the other person is already clear about the "what" you're referring to when using this pattern!

Structure

Phrase + 的

Examples

Note that for certain phrases, it may be ambiguous what the "what" refers to, and sometimes it could even refer to a "who."

- 妈妈做 的
  māma zuò de
  what mom cooks / cooked

- 我画 的
  wǒ huà de
  what I draw / drew
- 他写 的
  tā xiě de
  what he writes / wrote
- 你教 的
  nǐ jiāo de
  who/what you teach / taught

Similar to

- Expressing close possession without “de” (HSK1)
- Expressing possession with “de” (HSK1)
- Modifying nouns with adjective + “de” (HSK3)

Superlative "zui"

The most common way to form a superlative (best, worst, biggest, smallest, etc.) in Chinese is to use 最 (zuì) before an adjective (and a few select verbs).

最 (zuì) with Adjectives

Structure

The structure is:

And now you have the superlative form of the adjective. Unlike in English, this structure is consistent for all adjectives in Chinese. The inconsistencies in English sometimes confuse beginners, so note in the examples below how to say "best," "worst," "least," and "most" (meaning "greatest number").

Examples

- 哪个老师 最 好?

  Nǎge lǎoshī zuì hǎo?

  Which teacher is the best?
- 你们家谁 最 漂亮?

  Nǐmen jiā shéi zuì piàoliang?

  In your family who is the most beautiful?
- 谁 最 有钱?

  Shéi zuì yǒuqián?

  Who is the richest?
- 汉语 最 难。

  Hànyǔ zuì nán.

  The Chinese language is the most difficult.
- 这种事 最 麻烦。

  Zhè zhǒng shì zuì máfan.

  These kind of things are the most troublesome.

Optional 了 (le)

Occasionally you'll also see a 了 (le) added after the adjective. This simply adds emphasis to the "-est."

Structure

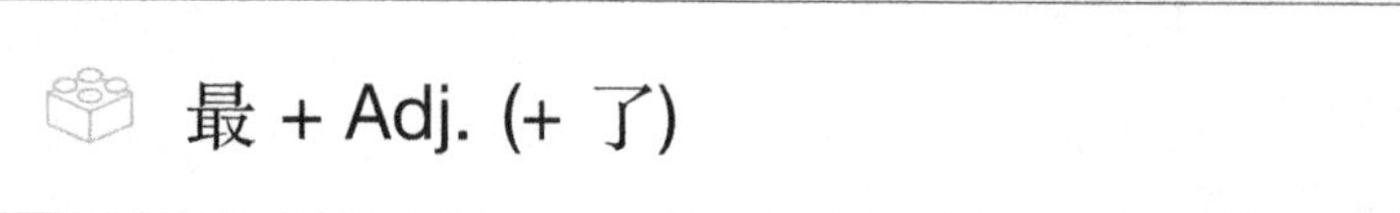

Examples

- 小狗最可爱了。 *This 了 is optional*
  Xiǎogǒu zuì kě'ài le.
  The puppy is the cutest.
- 四川菜最辣了。 *This 了 is optional*
  Sìchuān cài zuì là le.
  Sichuan food is the spiciest.
- 我的中国朋友最热情了。 *This 了 is optional*
  Wǒ de Zhōngguó péngyou zuì rèqíng le.
  My Chinese friend is the most enthusiastic.
- 他的学生最认真了。 *This 了 is optional*
  Tā de xuésheng zuì rènzhēn le.
  His student is the most serious.
- 黄山的风景最美了。 *This 了 is optional*
  Huángshān de fēngjǐng zuì měi le.
  Huang Mountain's landscape is the most beautiful.

最 (zuì) with Psychological Verbs

最 (zuì) can also come before psychological verbs, to express what one "most likes," "most hates," etc. It won't make sense if you try to use 最 (zuì) with non-psychological verbs, though.

Structure

The structure is:

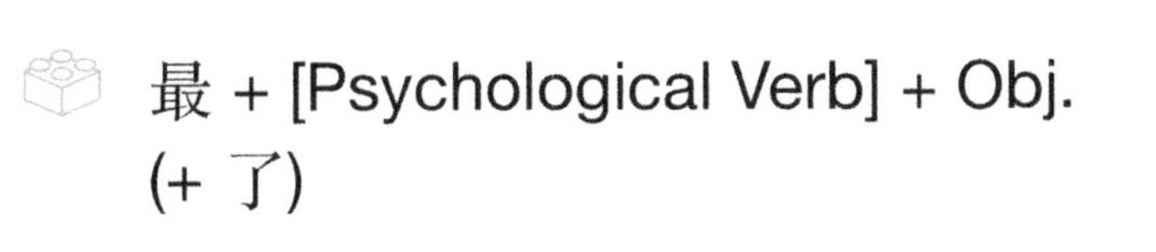

Note the 了 (le) on the end there! It's not strictly required, but you'll hear it a lot in spoken Chinese.

Examples

- 老板 最 喜欢 你了！
  Lǎobǎn zuì xǐhuan nǐ le!
  The boss likes you the best!
- 你 最 怕 什么？
  Nǐ zuì pà shénme?
  What do you most fear?
- 我 最 爱 中国菜。
  Wǒ zuì ài Zhōngguó cài.
  I love Chinese food most.
- 谁 最 了解 你？
  Shéi zuì liǎojiě nǐ?
  Who knows you best?
- 她 最 讨厌 抽烟的男人了。
  Tā zuì tǎoyàn chōuyān de nánrén le.
  She most hates men that smoke.

Although you could translate it as "like the best," pairing 最 (zuì) with the psychological verb 喜欢 (xǐhuan) is also a great way to talk about one's "favorite."

- 你 最 喜欢 什么颜色？
  Nǐ zuì xǐhuan shénme yánsè?
  What is your favorite color?

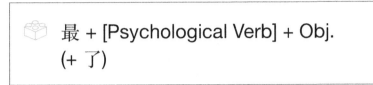

- 你 最 喜欢 什么动物？
  Nǐ zuì xǐhuan shénme dòngwù?
  What is your favorite animal?

Similar to

- Expressing “excessively” with “tai” (HSK1)
- Simple “noun + adjective” sentences (HSK1)
- Expressing “even more” with “geng” (HSK2), page 40
- Moderating positive adjectives with “hai” (HSK2), page 48
- Adjectives with “-ji le” (HSK3)
- Adjectives with “name” and “zheme” (HSK3)
- Intensifying with “duo” (HSK3)
- Special verbs with “hen” (HSK3)

The filler word "neige"

In conversation, you may find yourself at a loss for words, unable to find the correct phrase you are looking for, or simply needing time to gather your thoughts. When you experience this feeling, in English, you may say "umm" or "uhhh" or another filler word. In Chinese, the word for this is 那个 (nèige). (The word 那个 can be pronounced both "nàge" and "nèige," but for this usage, "nèige" is normally used.)

Structure

In English, words like "ummm" and "uh" are used as filler words when you're thinking about what to say. In Chinese, 那个 (nèige) is also used for this purpose. To English speakers not fortunate enough to be fluent in Mandarin this may raise an eyebrow because it can sound a bit "racist," but it's very common in Mandarin and you'll hear it quite often around Chinese speakers.

> (那个……) (那个……) + [anything] + (那个……)

那个 (nèige) can be inserted into sentences wherever you need to pause for thought.

Examples

- 那个 …… 我不跟你们一起去了，可以吗？
  Nèige ... wǒ bù gēn nǐmen yīqǐ qù le, kěyǐ ma?
  So, ummm... I won't go with you guys, OK?
- 我想吃 那个 …… 那个 …… 湖南菜。
  Wǒ xiǎng chī nèige ... nèige ... Húnán cài.
  I want to eat that... ummm, you know... Hunan cuisine.
- 那个 …… 我明天不来了。
  Nèige ... wǒ míngtiān bù lái le.
  Ummm... I'm not coming tomorrow.
- 那个 …… 这样做不好吧？
  Nèige ... zhèyàng zuò bù hǎo ba?
  Ummm, it's not good to do it this way?

- 那个 …… 你可以做我的女朋友吗?
  Nèige ... nǐ kěyǐ zuò wǒ de nǚpéngyou ma?
  Like... could you be my girlfriend?
- 那个 …… 不好意思，我要走了。
  Nèige ... bù hǎoyìsi, wǒ yào zǒu le.
  Ummmm... sorry, but I've gotta go.
- 她很漂亮，就像 那个 …… 明星一样。
  Tā hěn piàoliang, jiù xiàng nèige ... míngxīng yīyàng.
  She's very pretty, just like, you know, a celebrity.
- 我想看看你买的 那个 …… 那个 …… iPhone。
  Wǒ xiǎng kànkan nǐ mǎi de nèige ... nèige ... iPhone.
  I'd like to take a look at your, ummm, you know... iPhone you bought.
- 那个 …… 我要去开会了。
  Nèige ... wǒ yào qù kāihuì le.
  Ummm... I have to attend a meeting.
- 昨天 那个 …… 那个 …… 小笼包真好吃。
  Zuótiān nèige ... nèige ... xiǎolóngbāo zhēn hǎochī.
  Yesterday the, you know, steamed soup dumplings were so delicious.

Reduplication of measure words

If you know what a measure word is and how to use it, you may be ready for this pattern, where the measure word can repeat, or "reduplicate." It's not a terribly common structure, but the two most common examples of it are 个个 and 天天. It adds the meaning of "every" to the noun that follows.

Structure

The reduplicated measure word should precede the predicate of the sentence, often a verb phrase or an adjective.

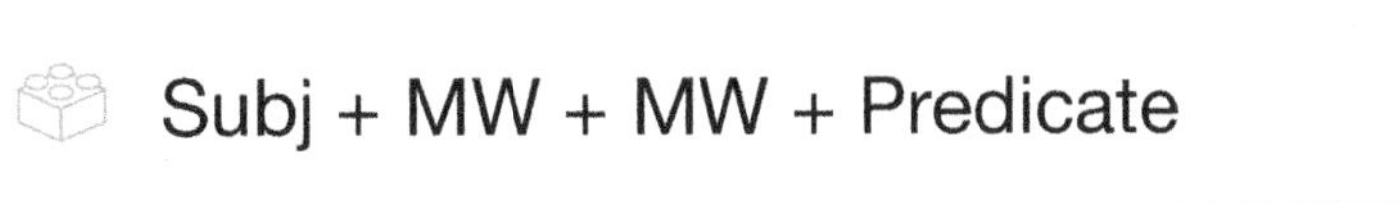

By far, the most commonly reduplicated measure words are 个个 (meaning "every one" of something) and 天天 (meaning "every day"). For less common measure words, the meaning is still the same: "every" of something (for which the measure word applies).

Examples

- 公司的员工 个个 都很好。
  Gōngsī de yuángōng gè gè dōu hěn hǎo.
- 他们 个个 都不喜欢打游戏。
  Tāmen gè gè dōu bù xǐhuan dǎ yóuxì.
- 这个星期他 天天 给我打电话。
  Zhège xīngqī tā tiān tiān gěi wǒ dǎ diànhuà.
- 我 天天 走路去公司。
  Wǒ tiān tiān zǒulù qù gōngsī.
- 现在 家家 都有手机。
  Xiànzài jiā jiā dōu yǒu shǒujī.

- 这里的公司 家家 都用苹果电脑。
  Zhèlǐ de gōngsī jiā jiā dōu yòng Píngguǒ diànnǎo.

- 我的衣服 件件 都很好看。
  Wǒ de yīfu jiàn jiàn dōu hěn hǎokàn.

- 这家店的书 本本 都很贵。
  Zhè jiā diàn de shū běn běn dōu hěn guì.

- 她 次次 都打车来。
  Tā cì cì dōu dǎchē lái.

- 这些小狗 只只 都很可爱。
  Zhèxiē xiǎogǒu zhī zhī dōu hěn kěài.

Similar to

- Reduplication of verbs (HSK2, HSK3), page 120
- Reduplication of adjectives (HSK3)

Expressing "when" with "de shihou"

In English, if we are reflecting on a past time, we often say, "*when* I was a child" or "*when* I was in school." In Chinese, this can also be expressed by using 的时候 (de shíhou).

Structure

To talk about events that happened *at* or *during* a particular time, 的时候 (de shíhou) is often used. This is simply attached to the word or phrase indicating the time:

(Subj.) + Verb / Adj. + 的时候, ...

As time words can appear before or after the subject, you can also place the "Time + 的时候 (de shíhou)" after the subject:

Time Word + 的时候, ...

Examples

- 你不在的时候，我会想你。
  Nǐ bù zài de shíhou, wǒ huì xiǎng nǐ.
  When you are not here, I'll miss you.
- 我上大学的时候，有很多朋友。
  Wǒ shàng dàxué de shíhou, yǒu hěn duō péngyou.
  When I was in college, I had a lot of friends.
- 上课的时候不要吃东西。
  Shàngkè de shíhou bùyào chī dōngxi.
  Don't eat when you are in class.
- 老板工作的时候喜欢喝咖啡。
  Lǎobǎn gōngzuò de shíhou xǐhuan hē kāfēi.
  When the boss works, he likes to drink coffee.

- 我 生气 的时候 ，请你不要笑。
  Wǒ shēngqì de shíhou , qǐng nǐ bùyào xiào.
  Please don't laugh when I'm angry.
- 妈妈 不在家 的时候 ，我自己做饭。
  Māma bù zài jiā de shíhou , wǒ zìjǐ zuòfàn.
  When mom is not home, I cook for myself.
- 开会 的时候 不要聊天。
  Kāihuì de shíhou bùyào liáotiān.
  Don't chat when you are in a meeting.
- 吃东西 的时候 不要说话。
  Chī dōngxi de shíhou bùyào shuōhuà.
  Don't talk when eating.
- 你 开车 的时候 会打电话吗?
  Nǐ kāichē de shíhou huì dǎ diànhuà ma?
  Do you talk on the phone when you're driving?
- 走路 的时候 不要玩手机。
  Zǒulù de shíhou bùyào wán shǒujī.
  Don't play with your phone while walking.

Similar to

- Expressing “when” with “shi” (HSK3)
- Simultaneous tasks with “yibian” (HSK3)

Indicating a number in excess

A number in excess of a certain amount is expressed by adding "多" (duō) to the end of a number. This is usually translated as "more than..." in English.

Structure

Number + 多 + [Measure word] (+ Noun)

Examples

- 我妈妈已经五十 多 岁了。
  Wǒ māma yǐjīng wǔshí duō suì le.
  My mother is over fifty.
- 我们走了两个 多 小时。
  Wǒmen zǒu le liǎng gè duō xiǎoshí.
  We walked for more than two hours.
- 这个班有两百 多 个学生。
  Zhège bān yǒu liǎng bǎi duō gè xuéshēng.
  There are more than two hundred students in this class.
- 这个包三万 多 块钱。
  Zhège bāo sān wàn duō kuài qián.
  This bag costs more than thirty thousand kuai.
- 这本书有一千 多 页。
  Zhè běn shū yǒu yī qiān duō yè.
  This book has more than a thousand pages.
- 他在国外住了二十 多 年了。
  Tā zài guówài zhù le èrshí duō nián le.
  He has been living abroad for more than twenty years.
- 他在那儿住了二十 多 天了。
  Tā zài nàr zhù le èrshí duō tiān le.
  He's been staying there for over 20 days.

- 我昨天收到了三十 多 条垃圾短信。

  Wǒ zuótiān shōudào le sānshí duō tiáo lājī duǎnxìn.

  I received more than thirty spam text messages yesterday.

- 这个城市有两千 多 年的历史。

  Zhège chéngshì yǒu liǎng qiān duō nián de lìshǐ.

  This city has a history of more than two thousand years.

In the above examples, 岁, 年 and 天 do not take a measure word.

When the number is smaller than eleven, the 多 can be put after the measure word. However, if the number is bigger than eleven, the 多 has to be put before the measure word:

✔ 五岁 多

wǔ suì duō

✘ 五十岁 多

wǔshí suì duō

✔ 五十 多 岁

wǔshí duō suì

✘ 九十块钱 多

jiǔshí kuàiqián duō

✔ 九十 多 块钱

jiǔshí duō kuàiqián

Similar to

- Asking about degree with "duo" (HSK1, HSK2), page 36
- Counting money (HSK1)
- Using "ji" to mean "several" (HSK2), page 65
- Approximating with sequential numbers (HSK3)
- Big numbers in Chinese (HSK3)
- Intensifying with "duo" (HSK3)
- Doing something more with "duo" (HSK4)

Using "ji" to mean "several"

One of the definitions of the common character 几 (jǐ) is "several," "a couple" or "a few." It's an uncertain number that is at least more than one, and probably less than five, but definitely less than ten.

几 (jǐ) as "a Few"

The simplest way to use 几 (jǐ) to mean "a few" is to use it directly with a measure word.

Structure

几 + Measure Word + Noun

Examples

- 桌子上有 几 本书。
  Zhuōzi shàng yǒu jǐ běn shū.
  There are a few books on the table.
- 只有 几 个人去过那个地方。
  Zhǐyǒu jǐ gè rén qù guo nàge dìfang.
  Only a few people have been to that place.
- 从上海到东京坐飞机只要 几 个小时。
  Cóng Shànghǎi dào Dōngjīng zuò fēijī zhǐ yào jǐ gè xiǎoshí.
  Flying from Shanghai to Tokyo only takes a few hours.
- 我每天都要喝 几 杯咖啡。
  Wǒ měi tiān dōu yào hē jǐ bēi kāfēi.
  Every day I have to drink a couple cups of coffee.
- 老板今天开了 几 个重要的会。
  Lǎobǎn jīntiān kāi le jǐ gè zhòngyào de huì.
  The boss had a few important meetings today.

几 (jǐ) as "a Few Tens"

It is similar to how in English we can say, "a few dozen" or "a couple dozen," though in this case instead of "twelves of something" we are saying "tens of something."

Structure

几 + 十 + Measure Word + Noun

Examples

- 他只想学 几十 个汉字。
  Tā zhǐ xiǎng xué jǐ shí gè Hànzì.
  He only wants to study a few dozen Chinese characters.
  "Dozens" is the closest we can get in natural English to the Chinese, which literally means "tens."
- 我们公司有 几十 个员工。
  Wǒmen gōngsī yǒu jǐ shí gè yuángōng.
  Our company has a few dozen employees.
- 他写过 几十 本书，我都喜欢。
  Tā xiě guo jǐ shí běn shū, wǒ dōu xǐhuan.
  He wrote a few dozen books. I like them all.
- 这个年轻的演员演了 几十 部电影。我都喜欢。
  Zhège niánqīng de yǎnyuán yǎn le jǐ shí bù diànyǐng. Wǒ dōu xǐhuan.
  This young actor has acted in dozens of movies. I like them all.
- 老板在国外有 几十 套房子。
  Lǎobǎn zài guówài yǒu jǐ shí tào fángzi.
  The boss has a few dozen houses abroad.

几 (jǐ) as "a Few Hundred / Thousand / Ten Thousand"

In Chinese we can put 几 (jǐ) together with 百 (bǎi), 千 (qiān), or 万 (wàn), just like how in English we might say, "a few hundred" or a "few thousand."

Structure

几 + 百 / 千 / 万 + Measure Word + Noun

Examples

- 妈妈每个月都给我 几百 块钱。
  Māma měi gè yuè dōu gěi wǒ jǐ bǎi kuài qián.
  Mom gives me a couple hundred dollars every month.
- 这个月我们卖了 几千 本书。
  Zhège yuè wǒmen mài le jǐ qiān běn shū.
  We sold a couple thousand books this month.
- 几百 家外国公司参加了这个大会。
  Jǐ bǎi jiā wàiguó gōngsī cānjiā le zhège dàhuì.
  Several hundred foreign companies attended this conference.
- 这篇文章有 几万 个字，太长了。
  Zhè piān wénzhāng yǒu jǐ wàn gè zì, tài cháng le.
  This article has tens of thousands of characters. It's too long.
- 我认识一个朋友，她有 几百 双鞋。
  Wǒ rènshi yī gè péngyou, tā yǒu jǐ bǎi shuāng xié.
  I have a friend that has a couple hundred pairs of shoes.

好几 (hǎojǐ) as "Quite a Few"

You can think of 好几 (hǎojǐ) as meaning "quite a few," usually in the range of five to ten.

Structure

好几 + Measure Word + Noun

Examples

- 他读了 好几 遍。
  Tā dú le hǎojǐ biàn.
  He's read quite a few times.
- 我有 好几 个室友。
  Wǒ yǒu hǎojǐ gè shìyǒu.
  I have quite a few roommates.

- 我奶奶有 好几 个孩子。
  Wǒ nǎinai yǒu hǎojǐ gè háizi.
  My grandma has quite a few children.
- 他吃了 好几 碗米饭。
  Tā chī le hǎojǐ wǎn mǐfàn.
  He ate quite a few bowls of rice.
- 我们去过 好几 次北京。
  Wǒmen qù guo hǎojǐ cì Běijīng.
  We've been to Beijing quite a few times.

Similar to

- Expressing "some" with "yixie" (HSK1)
- Indicating a number in excess (HSK2), page 63
- Using "youde" to mean "some" (HSK3)

Aspect particle "zhe"

The particle 着 (zhe) is one way of indicating the *continuous aspect* in Mandarin Chinese (another common way is using the adverb 在 in front of verbs). You may have heard that the Chinese particle 着 added onto the end of verbs is similar to the use of *-ing* in English. This isn't particularly helpful, however, because the use of 着 in Chinese is not nearly so commonly used, and can also be quite idiomatic.

Basic Usage

The main idea here is that the action won't just happen and stop immediately; it will continue for a while.

Structure

Examples

This basic pattern is often used with commands involving certain verbs where the action persists for a while.

- 我读，你听 着 。
  Wǒ dú, nǐ tīng zhe .
  I'll read, and you listen.
- 我们做，你们看 着 。
  Wǒmen zuò, nǐmen kàn zhe .
  We will do it, and you all watch.
- 你们坐 着 ，我马上回来。
  Nǐmen zuò zhe , wǒ mǎshàng huílái.
  Sit for a while. I'll be right back.
- 我出去一下，你帮我看 着 行李。
  Wǒ chūqù yīxià, nǐ bāng wǒ kān zhe xíngli.
  I'll go out for a second, and you watch the luggage for me.

Used for Manner or State in which an Action is Performed

This pattern is used when you want to use one verb to describe how *another* action is performed.

Structure

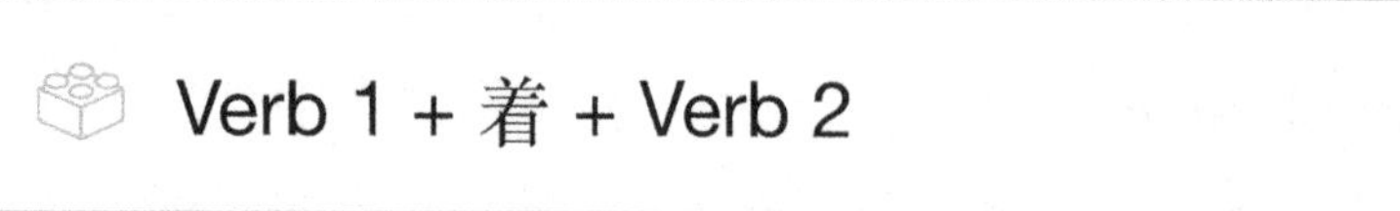

Note that the **first verb** (followed by 着) describes the **state**; the second verb is the action verb. In this case, the "-ing" translation can be useful for the state.

Examples

- 她喜欢站 着 吃饭。
  Tā xǐhuan zhàn zhe chīfàn.
  She likes to eat standing up.
  "standing + eat = eating while standing"
- 他笑 着 说"对不起"。
  Tā xiào zhe shuō "duìbuqǐ".
  Smiling, he said, "I'm sorry."
  "smiling + say = saying "I'm sorry" while smiling
- 孩子抱 着 爸爸哭了起来。
  Háizi bào zhe bàba kū le qǐlái.
  Hugging his daddy, the child started to cry.
  "hugging + cry = crying while hugging

Note: If you want to make a sentence where both verbs are action verbs (neither is truly a state), then you don't want this pattern; you want 一边……，一边…… (yībiān..., yībiān...).

Used for Continuous State

While it's true that the "full progressive pattern" can make use of 着, this is not a pattern you're going to want to use all the time.

Usage Examples

The verbs most commonly used with 着 are the ones below:

- 开 (kāi) alone can mean "to open" or "to turn on." Adding 着 allows one to express that something "is open" or "is on."
- 关 (guān) alone can mean "to close" or "to turn off." Adding 着 allows one to express that something "is closed" or "is off."

- 穿 (chuān) alone means "to wear." Adding 着 allows one to express that one "is wearing" something (on one's person).
- 戴 (dài) alone means "to wear" (an accessory). Adding 着 allows one to express that one "is wearing" a hat, jewelry, or accessory (on one's person).
- 躺 (tǎng) alone means "to lie on one's back." Adding 着 allows one to express that someone "is lying down."

Sentence Examples

✔ 公司的门开 着 ，可是没人在。
Gōngsī de mén kāi zhe, kěshì méi rén zài.
The office door is open but no one is in there.
"Being open" is a state, so using 着 is natural.)

✘ 公司的门 在 开，可是没人在。
Gōngsī de mén zài kāi, kěshì méi rén zài.
"Being open" is not an action, so don't use 在.)

✔ 她穿 着 一条小黑裙。
Tā chuān zhe yī tiáo xiǎo hēi qún.
She's wearing a little black dress.
"Be wearing" is a state, so using 着 is natural.)

✘ 她 在 穿一条小黑裙。
Tā zài chuān yī tiáo xiǎo hēi qún.
"Be wearing" is not an action, so don't use 在.)

✔ 躺 着 最舒服。
Tǎng zhe zuì shūfu.
It's most comfortable just lying down.
"Lying down" is a state, so using 着 is natural.)

✘ 在 躺最舒服。
Zài tǎng zuì shūfu.
"Lying here" is not strictly an action, so don't use 在.)

Colloquial Sayings

Certain verbs tend to take 着 more frequently than others, and what the 着 exactly is *doing* might not be apparent at all. It's best to think of these usages as set phrases.

Examples

- 听 着 ！
  Tīng zhe!
  "to listen and keep listening"
- 别客气，拿 着 吧。
  Bié kèqi, ná zhe ba.
  "to take and keep it"

- 你们等 着 ！
  Nǐmen děng zhe!
  "to wait and keeping waiting"

Verb + 着 + 玩 "For Fun"

There's also one colloquial usage of 着 that's often chosen for special treatment by Chinese textbooks, so we'll cover it here as well:

Subj. + 是 + Verb + 着 + 玩 + 的

This pattern may look like that "doing an action in a particular state" pattern already covered above, but in practice it doesn't really work that way. It just means "[Verb] for fun" or "[Verb] as a joke."

Examples of Verb + 着 + 玩

- 你不要生气，我是说 着 玩的。
  Nǐ bùyào shēngqì, wǒ shì shuō zhe wán de!
  Don't be mad. I was just joking.
- 我听不懂英文歌，只是听 着 玩的。
  Wǒ tīng bu dǒng Yīngwén gē, zhǐshì tīng zhe wán de.
  I don't understand English songs. I just listen to them for fun.

Similar to

- Expressing actions in progress with "zai" (HSK1)
- Alternative existential sentences (HSK3)
- Simultaneous tasks with "yibian" (HSK3)
- Using "zhe" when "verbing away" (HSK4)

Conceding with “ba”

The particle 吧 (ba) can also be used to *concede* a point. That is, 吧 (ba) can be used to accept or agree with something that you're not particularly happy about, the way we might use “all right” or “fine then” in English.

Structure

Similar to other uses of 吧 (ba), this usage is also simply placed on the end of a sentence or statement.

Statement + 吧

Examples

To understand what someone is conceding to, it's best to present this usage as a number of super short dialogs which provide a little context.

In this first one, B has to accept that his luxury goods shopping dreams have been shattered.

A: 太贵了！

Tài guì le!

That's too expensive!

B: 好 吧 ，我们可以看看别的。

Hǎo ba , wǒmen kěyǐ kànkan biéde.

All right, we can take a look at something else.

Now B must accept inconvenient schedule changes.

A: 下午我不在家，你可以晚上来吗?

Xiàwǔ wǒ bù zài jiā, nǐ kěyǐ wǎnshang lái ma?

This afternoon I won't be home. Can you come by this evening?

B: 行 吧 。

Xíng ba .

All right.

B is now conceding that going out in this crazy rain doesn't make sense.

A: 雨太大了，明天再去买吧。

Yǔ tài dà le, míngtiān zài qù mǎi ba.

It's raining heavily. Let's go buy it tomorrow.

B: 好 吧 ，但是明天一定要买到。

Hǎo ba, dànshì míngtiān yídìng yào mǎidào.

Fine, but tomorrow we definitely have to buy it.

Now B is agreeing to let more guys into his secret club.

A: 可以带朋友吗?

Kěyǐ dài péngyou ma ?

Can I bring friends?

B: 行 吧 ，但是不能带女孩。

Xíng ba, dànshì bù néng dài nǚhái.

All right, but you can't bring girls.

Now B is having a friend cancel plans on him. Not a good day for B!

A: 我今天不太舒服，你可以自己去吗?

Wǒ jīntiān bù tài shūfu, nǐ kěyǐ zìjǐ qù ma?

I'm not feeling well today. Can you go by yourself?

B: 好 吧 ，那你好好休息。

Hǎo ba, nà nǐ hǎohǎo xiūxi.

All right, rest well then.

Similar to

- Softening speech with “ba” (HSK1)
- Suggestions with “ba” (HSK1)
- Reviewing options with “ba” (HSK4)

Expressing "already" with just "le"

You understand the word 已经 (yǐjīng)[1] to mean "already" in Chinese, and it is followed with a 了 (le). However, sometimes, that feeling of "already" can also be expressed with 了 (le) alone if it is used in response to a preceding question or statement.

Structure

Subj. + [Verb Phrase] + 了

Examples

When "already" is implied using this structure, it is usually (if not always) in response to a preceding question or statement. Therefore, the following examples are in dialog format.

A: 老板呢？

Lǎobǎn ne?

Where is the boss?

B: 他走 了 。

Tā zǒu le .

He has (already) left.

A: 孩子还在上大学吗？

Háizi hái zài shàng dàxué ma?

Are your kids still in college?

B: 他们工作 了 。

Tāmen gōngzuò le .

They (already) work.

This expression emphasizes that they're not students anymore, and have already entered the workforce.

A: 用我的车吧？

Yòng wǒ de chē ba?

How about using my car?

---

1. Expressing "already" with "yijing" (Grammar), page 22

B: 谢谢，我们有车 了 。

Xièxie, wǒmen yǒu chē le.

Thanks. We (already) have a car.

A: 你要不要告诉他?

Nǐ yào bu yào gàosu tā?

Are you going to tell him?

B: 他知道 了 。

Tā zhīdào le.

He (already) knows.

A: 你应该问老师。

Nǐ yīnggāi wèn lǎoshī.

You should ask the teacher.

B: 我问 了 。

Wǒ wèn le.

I've (already) asked.

Similar to

- Expressing "already" with "dou" (HSK2), page 20
- Expressing "already" with "yijing" (HSK2), page 22

Expressing experiences with "guo"

The aspect particle 过 (guo) is used to indicate that an **action has been experienced** in the past.

Basic Usage

Structure

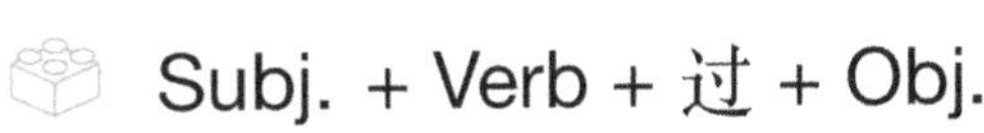

Subj. + Verb + 过 + Obj.

What this expresses is that the verb *has been* done at least once before, without specifying a particular time. 过 (guo) is used to talk about whether something has *ever* happened - whether it *has been experienced*.

Examples

In English, if you're asking a question and really trying to figure out if someone has *ever* done something before, we tend to use the words "ever" and "before." In Chinese, 过 (guo) alone expresses this, without the need for additional words.

- 你学 过 中文吗?
  Nǐ xué guo Zhōngwén ma?
  Have you ever studied Chinese?
- 你见 过 那个人吗?
  Nǐ jiàn guo nàge rén ma?
  Have you seen that person before?
- 我们来 过 这个地方。
  Wǒmen lái guo zhège dìfang.
  We've been to this place before.
- 我也吃 过 日本菜。
  Wǒ yě chī guo Rìběn cài.
  I've also eaten Japanese food before.
- 你看 过 这个电影吗?
  Nǐ kàn guo zhège diànyǐng ma?
  Have you seen this movie?

Negating a 过 (guo) Sentence

Because 过 (guo) is used to talk about past actions, it should be negated with 没 (méi).

Structure

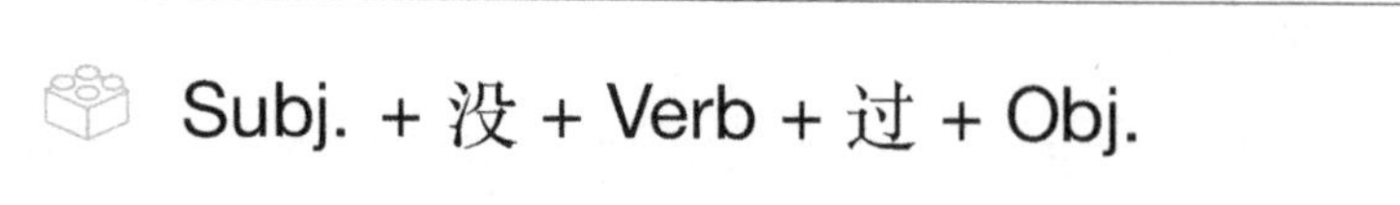

Examples

Note that when you translate these examples into English, "have *never*" [done something] is often more natural, indicating that someone *lacks the **experience** of having done something*, rather than just "have not" [done something].

- 我没想过这个问题。
  Wǒ méi xiǎng guo zhège wèntí.
  I've never thought about this question before.
- 我没学过这个词。
  Wǒ méi xué guo zhège cí.
  I have never studied this word before.
- 妈妈没买过很贵的衣服。
  Māma méi mǎi guo hěn guì de yīfu.
  Mom has never bought any expensive clothes before.
- 我们都没坐过飞机。
  Wǒmen dōu méi zuò guo fēijī.
  None of us has ever been on a airplane before.
- 你们没见过美女吗?
  Nǐmen méi jiàn guo měinǚ ma?
  Have you never seen beautiful girls before?

To emphasize "never" even more, you can also use the word 从来 (cónglái).

Using 过 (guo) with 了 (le)

You'll sometimes see 过 (guo) used together with 了 (le). This can be a little confusing, as it doesn't seem to be following the rules laid out above. For more on this special usage of 过 (guo), see the article on using 过 (guo) with 了 (le)[1].

Similar to

- Expressing completion with "le" (HSK1)
- Expressing "once" with "cengjing" (HSK5)
- Taiwanese "you" (HSK5)

1. Using "guo" with "le" (Grammar), page 82

Modal particle "ne"

You may have already learned how to ask questions with 呢 (ne), but did you know that it's also used in statements? In this usage, 呢 (ne) is imparting a certain "mood" (hence the word "modal") or "attitude." It's used when trying to sound more confident and convincing to someone else.

Structure

 Statement + 呢

Examples

For each of these examples, just a bit of context is needed to understand what the speaker is trying to convince someone of.

- 我不要回家。还早 呢 ！
  Wǒ bù yào huíjiā. Hái zǎo ne!
  I don't want to go home. It's still early!
- 太远了，坐火车要十个小时 呢 。
  Tài yuǎn le, zuò huǒchē yào shí gè xiǎoshí ne.
  .
- 他晚上十点才来 呢 。
  Tā wǎnshang shí diǎn cái lái ne.
  .
- 春节离我们还远 呢 。
  Chūnjié lí wǒmen hái yuǎn ne.
  .
- 你才跑了两百米，还有八百米 呢 。
  Nǐ cái pǎo le liǎng bǎi mǐ, háiyǒu bā bǎi mǐ ne.
  .
- 你还听这个歌 呢 。
  Nǐ hái tīng zhège gē ne.
  .

- 你怎么还在吃 呢 ?
  Nǐ zěnme hái zài chī ne.
  .
- 你喝吧，还有很多可乐 呢 。
  Nǐ hē ba, háiyǒu hěn duō kělè ne.
  .
- 雨还很大 呢 ，我们不要出去了。
  Yǔ hái hěn dà ne, wǒmen bù yào chūqù le .
  .
- 我找了你很久 呢 ，你去哪里了?
  Wǒ zhǎo le nǐ hěn jiǔ ne, nǐ qù nǎlǐ le?
  .

Similar to

- Questions with “ne” (HSK1, HSK3)
- Softening the tone of questions with “ne” (HSK5)

Using "guo" with "le"

You might be familiar with using 过 (guo) to indicate that an **action has been experienced** in the past[1], but then also see it used together with 了 (le). What's going on here? If you're already familiar with the basic usage of both 了 (le) and 过 (guo), then a special explanation of how they sometimes work together is now in order.

Basic Pattern

Structure

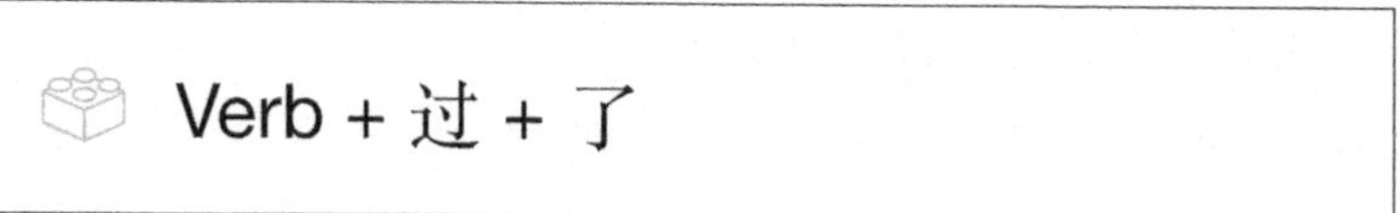

You'll notice that this pattern is often used for everyday behaviors. It's used for actions like "eating" and "brushing one's teeth" and "taking a shower."

Examples

- 她吃过了。
  Tā chī guo le.
  She has eaten (already).
- 牙刷过了。
  Yá shuā guo le.
  I've brushed my teeth (already).
- 洗过了。
  Xǐ guo le.
  I've showered (already).
- 我们看过了。
  Wǒmen kàn guo le.
  We've seen it (already).
- 他们见过了。
  Tāmen jiàn guo le.
  They've met (already).

---

1. Expressing experiences with "guo" (Grammar), page 77

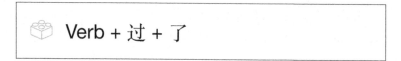

The Pattern with an Object

For the examples above, you could have inserted an object to modify the basic pattern, getting this:

> Verb + 过 + Obj. + 了

The object has been inserted in the sentences below:

- 你吃过饭了吗?
  Nǐ chī guo fàn le ma?
  Have you eaten (already)?
- 我刷过牙了。
  Wǒ shuā guo yá le.
  I have brushed my teeth (already).
- 他洗过澡了。
  Tā xǐ guo zǎo le.
  He has showered (already).
- 我给他打过电话了。
  Wǒ gěi tā dǎ guo diànhuà le.
  I called him (already).
- 客户看过合同了吗?
  Kèhù kàn guo hétong le ma?
  Has the client read the contract (already)?

What 过 (guo) Does

You would be right to point out that 过 (guo) is mainly used to call attention to the fact that someone *has had an* ***experience.*** This is the basic pattern pointed out in the article on the basic usage of the aspectual particle 过[1] (guo). In the examples above, though, it's not any "once-in-a-lifetime" *experiences* being expressed, it's more just the information that these actions are *done.* Here, 过 (guo) and 了 (le) work together to emphasize that an action is *already done.* This is why the translations on the side add the word "already" in parentheses at the end; this is the feeling the sentences give you. In fact, to emphasize

1. Expressing experiences with "guo" (Grammar), page 77

the idea of *already done* even further, you could add the word for "already," 已经 (yǐjīng), before the verbs in the examples below, and it also works just fine:

- 她 已经 吃 过 饭 了 。
  Tā yǐjīng chī guo fàn le.
  She has already eaten (a meal).
- 我 已经 刷 过 牙 了 。
  Wǒ yǐjīng shuā guo yá le.
  I have already brushed my teeth.
- 他 已经 洗 过 澡 了 。
  Tā yǐjīng xǐ guo zǎo le.
  He has already had a shower.

When to Use 过 (guo) with 了 (le)

So when would you use the sentences above? You'd be emphasizing that the action has *already* occurred (so it doesn't need to be done again), so it would probably be something like this:

For the eating example:

A: 她想吃饭吗?

Tā xiǎng chīfàn ma?

Does she want to eat?

B: 她 已经 吃 过 饭 了 。

Tā yǐjīng chī guo fàn le.

She has already eaten.

For the tooth brushing example:

A: 别忘记刷牙。

Bié wàngjì shuā yá.

Don't forget to brush your teeth.

B: 我 已经 刷 过 牙 了 。

Wǒ yǐjīng shuā guo yá le.

I have already brushed my teeth.

For the taking a shower example:

A: 他应该洗澡。

Tā yīnggāi xǐzǎo.

He should take a shower.

B: 他 已经 洗 过了 。

Tā yǐjīng xǐ guo le.

He has already showered.

Basic comparisons with "bi"

Also known as: 比字句 (bǐ zì jù).

One of the most common words when comparing things in Chinese is to use 比 (bǐ). 比 (bǐ) has similarities to the English word "than," but it requires a word order that's not so intuitive, so you'll want to practice it quite a bit.

Basic Usage

You could think of 比 (bǐ) as meaning "than," except that it sits between the two things being compared. The word order will take a little getting used to, but aside from that, the pattern is quite easy.

Structure

To say that one thing is more *adjective* than another, the structure is:

The noun that's placed first is the one that comes out on top in the comparison. So in the sentence:

- 小李 比 小张 高 。
  Xiǎo Lǐ bǐ Xiǎo Zhāng gāo .
  Xiao Li is taller than Xiao Zhang.

小李 (Xiǎo Lǐ) is taller. The same situation could be described as

- 小张 比 小李 矮 。
  Xiǎo Zhāng bǐ Xiǎo Lǐ ǎi .
  Xiao Zhang is shorter than Xiao Li.

Examples

- 他 比 老师 聪明 。
  Tā bǐ lǎoshī cōngming .
  He is smarter than the teacher.
- 上海 比 纽约 大 吗?
  Shànghǎi bǐ Niǔyuē dà ma?
  Is Shanghai bigger than New York?

- 她 比 她妈妈 漂亮 。
  Tā bǐ tā māma piàoliang .
  She is prettier than her mother.
- 星巴克的咖啡 比 这里的咖啡 贵 。
  Xīngbākè de kāfēi bǐ zhèlǐ de kāfēi guì .
  The coffee at Starbucks is more expensive than the coffee here.
- 地铁 比 公交车 方便 。
  Dìtiě bǐ gōngjiāochē fāngbiàn .
  The subway is more convenient than the bus.

Common Errors

Try not to make these mistakes:

很 (hěn) can't used in the comparison.

✘ 他 比 我 很高 。
Tā bǐ wǒ hěn gāo .

✔ 他 比 我 高 。
Tā bǐ wǒ gāo .
He's taller than me.

The adjective used in the comparison should be positive, not negative.

✘ 我 比 他 不高 。
Wǒ bǐ tā bù gāo .

✔ 他 比 我 高 。
Tā bǐ wǒ gāo .
He's taller than me.

比 (bǐ) is not used with 一样 (yīyàng). 比 (bǐ) is used when two things are *not* the same.

✘ 我 比 他 一样 高。
Wǒ bǐ tā yīyàng gāo.

✔ 我 跟 他 一样 高。
Wǒ gēn tā yīyàng gāo.
I'm as tall as him.

Pattern Using 比 (bǐ) and 更 (gèng)

This is a slight upgrade of the basic 比 (bǐ) comparison pattern, adding in 更 (gèng) before the adjective[1]. 更 (gèng) means "even more," so the idea is that while one thing is already quite [adjective], this other thing is ***even more*** [adjective]. Pretty simple!

Structure

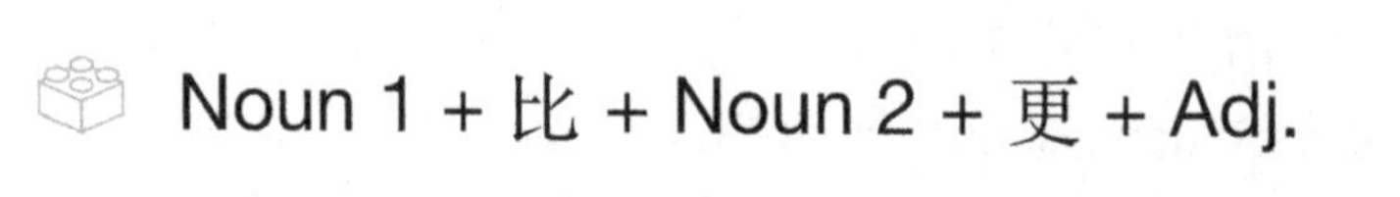

The only new thing here is the addition of 更 (gèng) before the adjective.

- 小李 比 小张 更高 。
  Xiǎo Lǐ bǐ Xiǎo Zhāng gèng gāo .
  Xiao Li is even taller than Xiao Zhang.

The implication is that while Xiao Zhang is *tall*, 小李 (Xiǎo Lǐ) is *even taller*.

Examples

- 我哥哥 比 我 更高 。
  Wǒ gēge bǐ wǒ gèng gāo .
  My big brother is even taller than me.
- 你男朋友 比 我男朋友 更帅 。
  Nǐ nánpéngyou bǐ wǒ nánpéngyou gèng shuài .
  Your boyfriend is even more handsome than mine.
- 这里的冬天 比 纽约的冬天 更冷 。
  Zhèlǐ de dōngtiān bǐ Niǔyuē de dōngtiān gèng lěng .
  The winter here is even colder than it is in New York.
- 中文语法 比 汉字 更好玩 。
  Zhōngwén yǔfǎ bǐ Hànzì gèng hǎowán .
  Chinese grammar is even more fun than Chinese characters.
- 你的问题 比 我的问题 更麻烦 。
  Nǐ de wèntí bǐ wǒ de wèntí gèng máfan .
  Your problem is even more troublesome than mine.

---

1. Expressing "even more" with "geng" (Grammar), page 40

Similar to

- Expressing "much more" in comparisons (HSK2, HSK3), page 205
- Basic comparisons with "meiyou" (HSK3)
- Basic comparisons with "yiyang" (HSK3)
- Expressing "even more" with "geng" or "hai" (HSK3)
- Expressing comparable degree with "you" (HSK3)
- Basic comparisons with "bu bi" (HSK5)

Expressing "for" with "gei"

The preposition 给 (gěi) can mean "for," as in, "everything I do, I do it *for* you." You can also think of it as meaning "give," like to give a service or to give something to someone. In this case, the default position of the character is before the verb, although it sometimes comes after, depending on the verb.

Structure

The meaning of 给 is very similar to 为 (wèi) in Chinese, but 给 is more informal than 为, and there are many cases where it's simply based on convention and general practice to decide to use one or the other.

Note that the "recipient" in the pattern above is usually a person but isn't necessarily a person. It could be an animal, company, or any number of other types of recipients.

Examples

- 给客人倒茶。
  Gěi kèrén dàochá.
  Pour tea for the guests.
- 妈妈在给孩子们做饭。
  Māma zài gěi háizi men zuòfàn.
  Mom cooks for the kids.
- 我儿子喜欢给小狗洗澡。
  Wǒ érzi xǐhuan gěi xiǎogǒu xǐzǎo.
  My son likes giving our dog a bath.
- 请给我拿一双筷子。
  Qǐng gěi wǒ ná yī shuāng kuàizi.
  Please get a pair of chopsticks for me.
- 可以给我买一杯咖啡吗?
  Kěyǐ gěi wǒ mǎi yī bēi kāfēi ma?
  Could you buy me a cup of coffee?

- 可以 给 我 拿一下 行李吗?
  Kěyǐ gěi wǒ ná yīxià xíngli ma?
  Can you take my luggage for me?
- 这个周末我们 给 儿子 开生日派对 。
  Zhège zhōumò wǒmen gěi érzi kāi shēngrì pàiduì .
  We're going to hold a birthday party for our son this weekend.
- 我没带钥匙，你能 给 我 开一下门 吗?
  Wǒ méi dài yàoshi, nǐ néng gěi wǒ kāi yīxià mén ma?
  I didn't bring the key. Could you open the door for me?
- 你想 给 我 打扫 房间吗?
  Nǐ xiǎng gěi wǒ dǎsǎo fángjiān ma?
  Would you like to clean the room for me?
- 如果你来中国玩，我 给 你 当导游 。
  Rúguǒ nǐ lái Zhōngguó wán, wǒ gěi nǐ dāng dǎoyóu .
  If you come visit China, I'll be your tour guide.

Similar to

- Using "dui" with verbs (HSK2), page 97
- Verbs followed by "gei" (HSK2), page 133
- Expressing "for" with "wei" (HSK5)

Expressing "from... to..." with "cong... dao..."

从……到……(cóng... dào...) is used in the same way as "from... to..." is used in English, and can be used both for times and places.

Used for Times

To express from one time to another, the following structure is used:

Structure

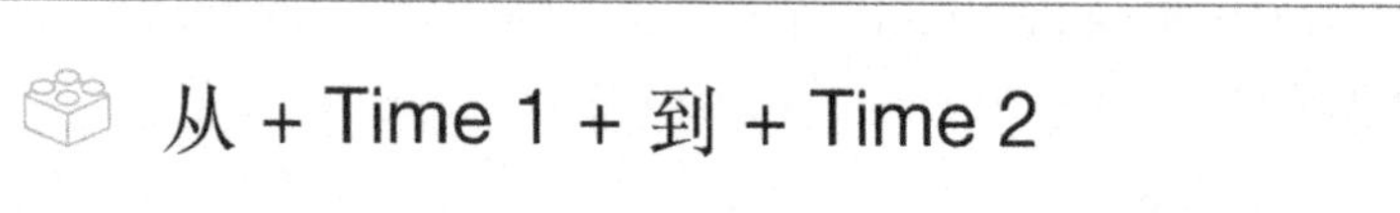

从 + Time 1 + 到 + Time 2

The "time" here does not necessarily have to be a standard time word; it can be any event or action.

Examples

- 从 2004 年 到 2008 年
  cóng èr-líng-líng-sì nián dào èr-líng-líng-bā nián
  from 2004 to 2008
- 从 一号 到 五号都在下雨。
  Cóng yī hào dào wǔ hào dōu zài xiàyǔ.
  From the first to the fifth, it's been raining non-stop.
- 老板 从 周二 到 周五都要出差。
  Lǎobǎn cóng Zhōuèr dào Zhōuwǔ dōu yào chūchāi.
  From Tuesday until Friday the boss will go on a business trip.
- 她 从 18 岁 到 现在都一个人住。
  Tā cóng shíbā suì dào xiànzài dōu yīgèrén zhù.
  She's lived alone since she was 18 until now.
- 你不能 从 早 到 晚不吃东西。
  Nǐ bù néng cóng zǎo dào wǎn bù chī dōngxi.
  You can't eat nothing from morning to night.

Remember that there are two options for the word order of time words.

Used for Places

The same structure can also be used to express "from" one place "to" another.

Structure

从 + Place 1 + 到 + Place 2

Examples

- 从 南京西路 到 南京东路
  cóng Nánjīng Xī Lù dào Nánjīng Dōng Lù
  from West Nanjing Road to East Nanjing Road
- 从 酒店 到 机场不太远。
  Cóng jiǔdiàn dào jīchǎng bù tài yuǎn.
  From the hotel to the airport is not too far.
- 从 上海 到 北京要几个小时。
  Cóng Shànghǎi dào Běijīng yào jǐ gè xiǎoshí.
  From Shanghai to Beijing it takes a few hours.
- 从 你家 到 机场可以坐地铁吗?
  Cóng nǐ jiā dào jīchǎng kěyǐ zuò dìtiě ma?
  From your place to the airport, can I take the subway?
- 从 这里 到 我们公司，你会看见很多美女。
  Cóng zhèlǐ dào wǒmen gōngsī, nǐ huì kànjiàn hěn duō měinǚ.
  From here to our company, you'll see many beautiful girls.

Similar to

- Expressing distance with “li” (HSK2), page 45
- Comparing “li” and “cong” (HSK4)
- Expressing “from (a certain time) on” using “zi……qi”
- Expressing “to come from” with “laizi” (HSK4)
- Expressing “until” with “dao” (HSK4)
- Expressing “from” with “cong… zhong” (HSK5)

Expressing "toward" with "wang"

Although 往 (wǎng) simply means "towards," it's not used as often as certain other prepositions and also has a few special use cases, so it warrants a little extra attention.

Used as "Towards"

往 (wǎng) is a preposition that means "towards" and precedes the verb it modifies.

Used before a Verb

This is the common one used in everyday speech.

Structure

Adding 往 (wǎng) with a location or place word indicates the direction of an action. Remember that the verb comes *after* this 往 phrase.

 往 + Direction / Place + Verb

Examples

- 一直往前走。
  Yīzhí wǎng qián zǒu.
  Go straight ahead.
- 往左拐。
  Wǎng zuǒ guǎi.
  Turn left.
- 往上看。
  Wǎng shàng kàn.
  Look up there.
- 那个小偷往东跑了。
  Nàge xiǎotōu wǎng dōng pǎo le.
  That thief ran towards the east.
- 不要往楼下扔垃圾。
  Bùyào wǎng lóuxià rēng lājī.
  Don't throw trash downstairs.

- 不要往小孩嘴巴里塞东西了！
  Bùyào wǎng xiǎohái zuǐba lǐ sāi dōngxi le!
  Stop stuffing food in the kid's mouth!

Used after a Verb

In written language, 往 (wǎng) can also be used *after* a few monosyllabic verbs, which are then followed by location nouns.

Structure

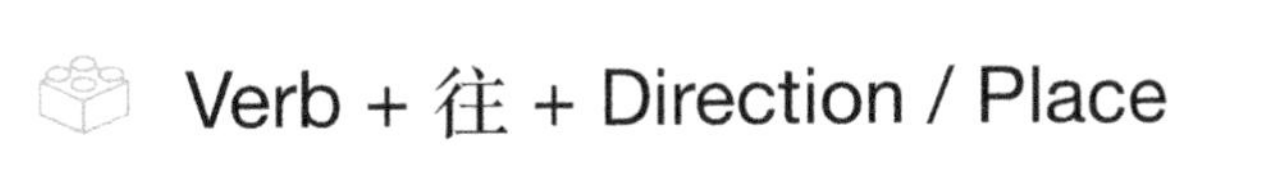

Verb + 往 + Direction / Place

Examples

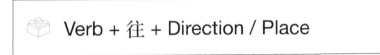

- 开往北京的火车
  kāi wǎng Běijīng de huǒchē
  the train that goes to Beijing
- 飞往纽约的飞机
  fēi wǎng Niǔyuē de fēijī
  the airplane that flies to New York
- 运往国外的货物
  yùn wǎng guówài de huòwù
  cargo that is shipped overseas

往下 as "Keep Going"

往下 (wǎng xià) expresses "keep going," implying that the process has been interrupted before. The verbs that follow are usually communication or sensory verbs: speak (说), read (读), write (写), watch (看), and listen (听) are common.

Examples

- 往下说。
  Wǎng xià shuō.
  Keep talking.
- 往下读。
  Wǎng xià dú.
  Keep reading.

- 你往下看就知道了。
  Nǐ wǎng xià kàn jiù zhīdào le.
  Keep reading and you'll see.

Similar to

- Expressing "towards" with "xiang" (HSK3)
- Comparing "chao" "xiang" and "wang" (HSK5)

Using "dui" with verbs

When using 对 (duì) as a preposition, it means "to" or "towards" an object or target. As with all prepositions, you've got to watch out when using this word, as usage of 对 in Chinese doesn't always totally "make sense" or correspond to English at all.

Basic Usage

Structure

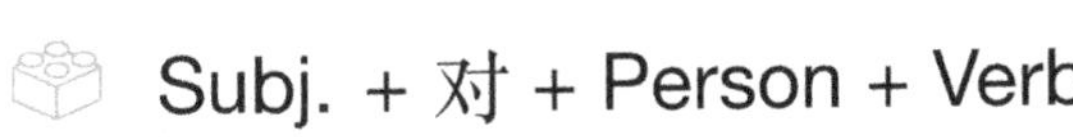

Subj. + 对 + Person + Verb

Note that you shouldn't be plugging in just any old verb here; the ones that work with 对 are limited.

Examples

- 宝宝对我笑了。
  Bǎobao duì wǒ xiào le.
  The baby smiled at me.
- 小狗在对你叫。
  Xiǎogǒu zài duì nǐ jiào.
  The dog is barking at you.
- 你不应该这样对父母说话。
  Nǐ bù yīnggāi zhèyàng duì fùmǔ shuōhuà.
  You shouldn't talk to your parents this way.
- 他总是对老师撒谎。
  Tā zǒngshì duì lǎoshī sāhuǎng.
  He always lies to his teachers.
- 不要对孩子发脾气。
  Bùyào duì háizi fā píqi.
  Don't lose your temper with the child.

Colloquial Expression 对……来说

In English we often start sentences with "to someone" or "for someone" when sharing that person's perspective. In Chinese, the pattern is:

 对 + Person + 来说，……

While this pattern was too common to omit from this page, it's covered in more depth as part of phrases using "laishuo."

Usage with Specific Verbs

Certain verbs, especially psychological verbs, are often used with 对, which means 对 is needed if you want to add an object into the structure. I good example is 对…… 感兴趣 ("to be interested in..."). In this case, 对 means "in," "on," "about," etc., and the object doesn't have to be a person. The short list below will give a few more verbs frequently paired with 对.

Structures

- 对…… 有兴趣 (yǒu xìngqù) to have an interest in...
- 对…… 感兴趣 (gǎn xìngqù) to feel interested in...
- 对…… 负责 (fùzé) to be responsible for...
- 对…… 满意 (mǎnyì) to feel satisfied with...
- 对…… 失望 (shīwàng) to be disappointed in/with...
- 对…… 好奇 (hàoqí) to be curious about...

Examples

Some example sentences:

- 我儿子 对 学外语很 感兴趣 。
  Wǒ érzi duì xué wàiyǔ hěn gǎn xìngqù .
  My son is very interested in learning foreign languages.
- 你应该 对 自己的工作 负责 。
  Nǐ yīnggāi duì zìjǐ de gōngzuò fùzé .
  You should be responsible for your job.
- 老板 对 你不太 满意 。
  Lǎobǎn duì nǐ bù tài mǎnyì .
  The boss is not very satisfied with you.
- 观众 对 比赛结果非常 失望 。
  Guānzhòng duì bǐsài jiéguǒ fēicháng shīwàng .
  The audience is very disappointed with the result of the game.

- 我的小女儿 对 所有动物都很 好奇 。
  Wǒ de xiǎo nǚ'ér duì suǒyǒu dòngwù dōu hěn hàoqí .
  My younger daughter is curious about all animals.

Similar to

- Expressing "for" with "gei" (HSK2), page 90
- Expressing "toward" with "wang" (HSK2), page 94
- Verbs followed by "gei" (HSK2), page 133
- Verbs preceded by "gei" (HSK2), page 136
- Expressing "towards" with "xiang" (HSK3)
- Comparing "dui" and "duiyu" (HSK5)
- Comparing "gen" and "dui" (HSK5)
- Expressing "for···" with "eryan" (HSK5)

Using the verb "xing"

The verb 姓 (xìng) literally means "to be surnamed" or "to have the surname." It may seem awkward at first that there's a verb just for this, but you'll find that it's used quite often in Chinese.

Giving One's Surname

姓 (xìng) is used most often to tell someone your own surname ("family name" or "last name"), or to ask the surname of someone else.

Structure

Examples

- 我 姓 王。
  Wǒ xìng Wáng.
  My family name is Wang.
- 你老板 姓 李吗?
  Nǐ lǎobǎn xìng Lǐ ma?
  Is your boss's last name Li?
- 那个帅哥 姓 张。
  Nàge shuàigē xìng Zhāng.
  That handsome guy's last name is Zhang.
- 我爸爸 姓 周，我妈妈 姓 林。
  Wǒ bàba xìng Zhōu, wǒ māma xìng Lín.
  My father's family name is Zhou. My mother's family name is Lin.
- 他女朋友 姓 钱。
  Tā nǚpéngyou xìng Qián.
  His girlfriend's last name is Qian.
- 你好，我 姓 毛。
  Nǐ hǎo, wǒ xìng Máo.
  Hello. My last name is Mao.

- 我 姓 赵，我太太也 姓 赵。

  Wǒ xìng Zhào, wǒ tàitai yě xìng Zhào.

  My last name is Zhao. My wife's last name is also Zhao.

- 我的中文老师 姓 陈。

  Wǒ de Zhōngwén lǎoshī xìng Chén.

  My Chinese teacher's surname is Chen.

- 你奶奶也 姓 陈吗?

  Nǐ nǎinai yě xìng Chén ma?

  Is your grandma's family name also Chen?

- 他们都 姓 李。

  Tāmen dōu xìng Lǐ.

  All of their surnames are Li.

Asking Someone's Surname

You can also use 姓 (xìng) to ask people their surnames. You could do this quite directly by saying:

- 你姓什么?

  Nǐ xìng shénme?

  What is your last name?

However, the formal way to ask has a set form:

- 您贵姓?

  Nín guì xìng?

  What is your honorable surname?

Literally this means "What is your honorable surname?" Use this form to be polite when asking people their surnames.

Similar to

- Using the verb "jiao" (HSK1)

Auxiliary verb "yao" and its multiple meanings

You probably already know the basic meaning of 要 (yào)[1] as "to want." It is actually a quite versatile word, though, and can also take on the meanings of "to need" as well as "will (do something)." In every case, context is crucial for figuring out which meaning someone is trying to express.

要 (yào) as "Want"

This structure could be used when ordering food at a restaurant or a shop. Here, it's being used for saying that you want *something.*

Structure

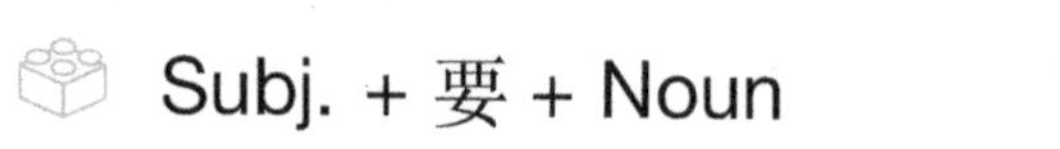

Examples

- 你 要 什么？
  Nǐ yào shénme?
  What do you want?
- 我 要 一杯水。
  Wǒ yào yī bēi shuǐ.
  I want a cup of water.
- 你们都 要 冰可乐吗？
  Nǐmen dōu yào bīng kělè ma?
  Do you all want coke with ice?
- 你 要 茶还是咖啡？
  Nǐ yào chá háishì kāfēi?
  Do you want tea or coffee?
- 我们 要 三碗米饭。
  Wǒmen yào sān wǎn mǐfàn.
  We want three bowls of rice.

---

1. Wanting to do something with "yao" (Grammar), page 110

要 (yào) as "Want to"

In Chinese, 要 (yào) can mean "want to" (similar to 想 (xiǎng)), but its tone is quite firm. So it's used for saying that you want ***to do** something*.

Structure

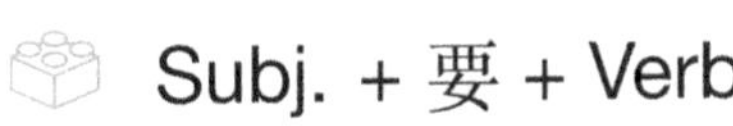

Subj. + 要 + Verb

Examples

- 你 要 喝什么酒?
  Nǐ yào hē shénme jiǔ?
  What kind of wine do you want to drink?
- 爸爸 要 买一个新手机。
  Bàba yào mǎi yī gè xīn shǒujī.
  Dad wants to buy a new cell phone.
- 我 要 跟你一起去。
  Wǒ yào gēn nǐ yīqǐ qù.
  I want to go with you.
- 她 要 去大城市找工作。
  Tā yào qù dà chéngshì zhǎo gōngzuò.
  She wants to go to a big city to find a job.
- 周末你们 要 一起看电影吗?
  Zhōumò nǐmen yào yīqǐ kàn diànyǐng ma?
  Do you want to go see a movie together this weekend?

要 (yào) as "Need to"

If you crank the urgency of "to want" up a few notches, you get "to need." The two meanings overlap, creating a fuzzy, "needy" gray area.

Structure

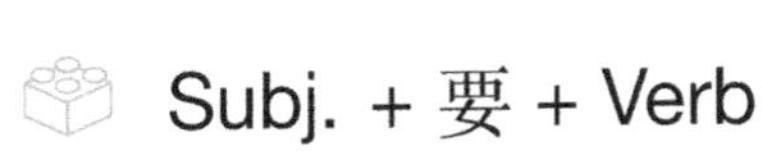

Subj. + 要 + Verb

Examples

- 你 要 早点睡觉。
  Nǐ yào zǎo diǎn shuìjiào.
  You need to go to bed earlier.
- 我们明天 要 上班。
  Wǒmen míngtiān yào shàngbān.
  We need to work tomorrow.

  logically, most people don't really WANT to work
- 老板今天 要 见一个新客户。
  Lǎobǎn jīntiān yào jiàn yī gè xīn kèhù.
  Today the boss needs to see a new client.
- 老师太累了，要 好好休息。
  Lǎoshī tài lèi le, yào hǎohǎo xiūxi.
  The teacher is too tired. She needs to rest well.
- 明天下雨，你 要 带伞。
  Míngtiān xiàyǔ, nǐ yào dài sǎn.
  It's going to rain tomorrow; you need to bring an umbrella.

要 (yào) as "Going to"

This use of 要 (yào) is like "going to" (similar to 会 (huì)).

Structure

Again, no change to the structure here, but it often includes a mention of a time *when* something is *going to happen*.

Subj. + 要 + Verb

If you want to know more about the related pattern "要…… 了" (yào… le), please see the "kuai… le" pattern[1].

1. Expressing "about to happen" with "le" (Grammar), page 188

Examples

- 星期五我们 要 开会。
  Xīngqīwǔ wǒmen yào kāihuì.
  We are going to have a meeting on Friday.
- 12 点我 要 去吃饭。
  Shí'èr diǎn wǒ yào qù chīfàn.
  I am going to go eat at 12 o'clock.
- 老板下周 要 出差吗?
  Lǎobǎn xià zhōu yào chūchāi ma?
  Is the boss going on a business trip next week?
- 他们明年 要 结婚了。
  Tāmen míngnián yào jiéhūn le.
  They are going to get married next year.
- 今年你 要 回家过年吗?
  Jīnnián nǐ yào huíjiā guònián ma?
  Are you going to return home this year to celebrate the Chinese New Year?

Context, Context, Context

You may have noticed that the meanings can easily overlap. To figure out what is intended, you need to use context. How urgent is the situation? is it likely to be something the speaker really *wants* to do? is it something that's totally *going to* happen, regardless of anyone's preference? Most often, a little background knowledge and some common sense are all you need to figure it out.

Similar to

- Expressing "about to happen" with "le" (HSK2), page 188
- Expressing "about to" with "jiuyao" (HSK2), page 14
- Wanting to do something with "yao" (HSK2), page 110
- Expressing "don't need to" with "buyong" (HSK4)
- Adding emphasis with "fei....buke" (HSK6)

Expressing "be going to" with "yao"

The auxiliary verb 要 (yào) has several different meanings[1], and here we'll tackle the "be going to" meaning. You'll use this when you are discussing your plans with someone.

Structure

The idea behind this usage of 要 (yào) is that someone is "planning to" or "going to" or "preparing to" do something. It's not that they just *want to*, or *have to*, it's that they fully expect to do it. It's in their plan.

This usage of 要 (yào) typically includes a time word of some sort, which may be placed before or after the subject. This is fairly logical; if you're discussing plans for the future, you're quite likely to say when you plan to do things.

Subj. + Time + 要 + Verb

Time + Subj. + 要 + Verb

Note that the time word is not strictly required, and when it's missing, you may at first find yourself wondering which usage of 要 (yào)[1] you're dealing with. This is normal; it just takes some getting used to.

Examples

- 我 明天 要 买一个 iPhone。
  Wǒ míngtiān yào mǎi yī gè iPhone.
  I am going to buy an iPhone tomorrow.
- 你们 现在 要 出去吗?
  Nǐmen xiànzài yào chūqù ma?
  Are you all going out now?
- 我们 今年 要 去美国。
  Wǒmen jīnnián yào qù Měiguó.
  We are planning to go to the U.S. this year.

1. Auxiliary verb "yao" and its multiple meanings (Grammar), page 102

- 他 下个月 要 来中国工作。
  Tā xià gè yuè yào lái Zhōngguó gōngzuò.
  He is coming to China to work next month.
- 你 下个星期 要 去她家吃晚饭吗?
  Nǐ xià gè xīngqī yào qù tā jiā chī wǎnfàn ma?
  Are you going to her place for dinner next week?
- 这个 星期天 你 要 做什么?
  Zhège Xīngqītiān nǐ yào zuò shénme?
  What are you doing this Sunday?
- 我 晚上 要 给妈妈打电话。
  Wǒ wǎnshang yào gěi māma dǎ diànhuà.
  I am going to call my mom this evening.
- 下午 老师 要 来我家。
  Xiàwǔ lǎoshī yào lái wǒ jiā.
  The teacher is coming to my place this afternoon.
- 老板 明天 要 见他们吗?
  Lǎobǎn míngtiān yào jiàn tāmen ma?
  Is the boss going to meet them tomorrow?
- 下班以后 你 要 回家吗?
  Xiàbān yǐhòu nǐ yào huíjiā ma?
  Are you planning to go home after getting off work?

Similar to

- Expressing "would like to" with "xiang" (HSK1)
- Expressing "about to happen" with "le" (HSK2), page 188
- Expressing "about to" with "jiuyao" (HSK2), page 14

Expressing permission with "keyi"

可以 (kěyǐ) is an auxiliary verb primarily used for expressing permission. It's often translated as "can," but in order to not get it confused with other words, it's best to think of it as "may" to emphasize the *permission* aspect.

Basic Usage

Just put 可以 (kěyǐ) in directly before a verb to create a meaning of "may" (plus the verb). It's the same structure whether it's a statement or a question.

Structure

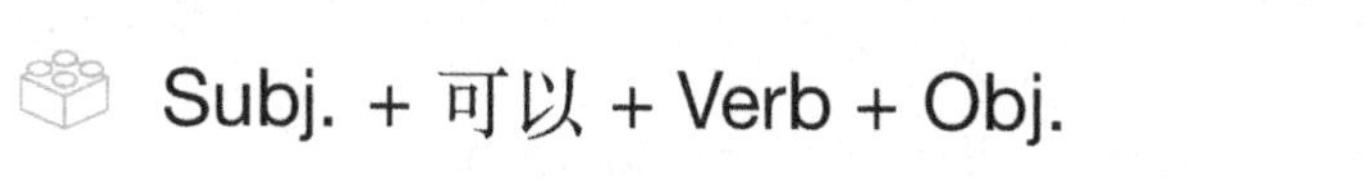

Use this structure to express permission to do things.

Examples

- 我 可以 进来吗?
  Wǒ kěyǐ jìnlái ma?
  May I come in?
- 二十一岁以后 可以 喝酒。
  Èrshí-yī suì yǐhòu kěyǐ hējiǔ.
  After you are 21 years old, you may drink alcohol.
- 妈妈，我 可以 出去玩吗?
  Māma, wǒ kěyǐ chūqù wán ma?
  Mom, may I go out and play?
- 我们 可以 在办公室吃饭吗?
  Wǒmen kěyǐ zài bàngōngshì chīfàn ma?
  Can we eat in the office?
- 我 可以 在这里停车吗?
  Wǒ kěyǐ zài zhèlǐ tíngchē ma?
  Can I park here?

Negating 可以 (kěyǐ) Sentences

可以 (kěyǐ) sentences are negated with 不 (bù), which is inserted before 可以 (kěyǐ).

Structure

 Subj. + 不 + 可以 + Verb + Obj.

Examples

- 孩子 不可以 看这个。
  Háizi bù kěyǐ kàn zhège.
  Children can't watch this.
- 你现在 不可以 进去。
  Nǐ xiànzài bù kěyǐ jìnqù.
  You can't go in right now.
- 这里 不可以 抽烟。
  Zhèlǐ bù kěyǐ chōuyān.
  You can't smoke here.
- 我们都 不可以 去。
  Wǒmen dōu bù kěyǐ qù.
  None of us may go.
- 你 不可以 说脏话。
  Nǐ bù kěyǐ shuō zānghuà.
  You can't say swear words.

Similar to

- Expressing ability or possibility with “neng” (HSK1)

Wanting to do something with "yao"

The auxiliary verb 要 (yào) has several different meanings[1], and here we'll tackle the "want to" meaning. To express "wanting to do" something, use 要 (yào) before the verb.

Structure

The verb 要 (yào) can be used as an auxiliary verb to indicate *wanting to do* something.

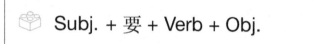

 Subj. + 要 + Verb + Obj.

Examples

- 他 要 学中文。
  Tā yào xué Zhōngwén.
  He wants to study Chinese.
- 宝宝 要 睡觉。
  Bǎobao yào shuìjiào.
  The baby wants to sleep.
- 早饭我 要 吃肉。
  Zǎofàn wǒ yào chī ròu.
  For breakfast I want to eat meat.
- 今天很累，我 要 休息。
  Jīntiān hěn lèi, wǒ yào xiūxi.
  Today I'm very tired. I want to rest.
- 这个周末你们 要 做什么？
  Zhège zhōumò nǐmen yào zuò shénme?
  This weekend what do you want to do?

1. Auxiliary verb "yao" and its multiple meanings (Grammar), page 102

要 (yào) and 想 (xiǎng)

Instead of using 要 (yào), it is also possible to use the word 想 (xiǎng). These two words are largely interchangeable, and both can mean "to want." The small difference is that 要 (yào) is often used for something you want to or *need* to do, and *plan to take action on*. It can sound a bit more demanding (and less polite). 想 (xiǎng) on the other hand, often conveys an idea on one's mind, that one *may or may not take action on*. You can think of it as meaning "would like to."

Examples

- 我 要 喝咖啡。
  Wǒ yào hē kāfēi.
  I want to drink coffee.
  I am going to get my hands on some coffee
- 我 想 喝咖啡。
  Wǒ xiǎng hē kāfēi.
  I'd like to drink coffee.
  I want to drink a cup of coffee, but may or may not act on that
- 你 要 吃什么?
  Nǐ yào chī shénme?
  What do you want to eat?
- 你 想 吃什么?
  Nǐ xiǎng chī shénme?
  What would you like to eat?

Similar to

- Expressing "will" with "hui" (HSK1)
- Expressing "would like to" with "xiang" (HSK1)
- Time words and word order (HSK1)
- Auxiliary verb "yao" and its multiple meanings (HSK2), page 102
- Comparing "yao" and "xiang" (HSK2), page 215
- Expressing "should" with "yinggai" (HSK3)
- Expressing future with "jiang" (HSK5)

Actions in a row

Linking actions together in a sentence is very straightforward and to the point. Because of this, there is no new word or phrase needed!

Structure

In Chinese, it's very easy to describe two actions in a row. Simply place one verb phrase after another, in this structure:

Subj. + [Verb Phrase 1] + [Verb Phrase 2]

No connecting word is needed. A common mistake in the early stages of learning Chinese is to try and link verbs with 和 (hé). This is incorrect; 和 (hé) is for linking nouns. Just use one verb phrase after another and the sequence of events is clear.

Examples

- 我要回家吃饭。
  Wǒ yào huí jiā chī fàn.
  I want to go home and eat.
- 你要去超市买东西吗?
  Nǐ yào qù chāoshì mǎi dōngxi ma?
  Are you going to the supermarket to buy things?
- 他不想去图书馆看书。
  Tā bù xiǎng qù túshūguǎn kàn shū.
  He doesn't want to go to the library and read.
- 你打电话告诉他了吗?
  Nǐ dǎ diànhuà gàosu tā le ma?
  Did you call and tell him?
- 我们要坐飞机去美国。
  Wǒmen yào zuò fēijī qù Měiguó.
  We are going to take an airplane to go to the USA.

- 你们可以 上 网 买 机票吗?
  Nǐmen kěyǐ shàng wǎng mǎi jīpiào ma?
  Can you use the Internet to buy airplane tickets?
- 老板下周 去 北京 开 会。
  Lǎobǎn xià zhōu qù Běijīng kāi huì.
  Next week the boss will go to Beijing to have a meeting.
- 中国人都要 回 家 过 年。
  Zhōngguó rén dōu yào huí jiā guò nián.
  Chinese people all go back home for Chinese New Year.
- 周末我喜欢自己 买 菜 做 饭。
  Zhōumò wǒ xǐhuan zìjǐ mǎi cài zuò fàn.
  I like to buy food to cook for myself on the weekend.
- 早上我先 刷 牙 洗 脸，再吃早饭。
  Zǎoshang wǒ xiān shuā yá xǐ liǎn, zài chī zǎofàn.
  In the morning, I first brush my teeth and wash my face, and then I eat breakfast.

Note that the English translations of these sentences use the word “and,” but there is no equivalent to it in Chinese.

Similar to

- Basic sentence order (HSK1)
- Events in quick succession with “yi… jiu…” (HSK4)

Expressing "together" with "yiqi"

If you want to express that you are doing something *together* with someone else, 一起 (yīqǐ) is your word!

Note: The pinyin for 一起 is written "yīqǐ" but pronounced "yìqǐ" due to a tone change rule.

Structure

一起 (yīqǐ) is the easiest way to express an action being done together with other people.

Subj. + 一起 + Verb + Obj.

The subject must be plural - a plural noun or two or more nouns linked with a conjunction. You can't do things together on your own, after all.

Examples

- 我们 一起 吃晚饭吧。
  Wǒmen yīqǐ chī wǎnfàn ba.
  Let's eat dinner together.
- 早上我和老公 一起 去上班。
  Zǎoshang wǒ hé lǎogōng yīqǐ qù shàngbān.
  In the morning, I go to work together with my husband.
- 周末我们 一起 去看电影，好吗？
  Zhōumò wǒmen yīqǐ qù kàn diànyǐng, hǎo ma?
  Let's go to the movies this weekend, shall we?
- 这两个公司 一起 做这个产品。
  Zhè liǎng gè gōngsī yīqǐ zuò zhège chǎnpǐn.
  These two businesses made this product together.
- 下班以后，你们 一起 来我家吧。
  Xiàbān yǐhòu, nǐmen yīqǐ lái wǒ jiā ba.
  After work, why don't you all come to my home together?

- 下个月我和妈妈 一起 去旅行。
  Xià gè yuè wǒ hé māma yīqǐ qù lǚxíng.
  Next month I'll go on a trip together with mom.
- 你们有没有 一起 玩过这个游戏？
  Nǐmen yǒu méiyǒu yīqǐ wán guo zhège yóuxì?
  Have you all ever played this game together?
- 他想和他太太 一起 学中文。
  Tā xiǎng hé tā tàitai yīqǐ xué Zhōngwén.
  He wants to study Chinese together with his wife.
- 结婚以后，你和父母会 一起 住吗？
  Jiéhūn yǐhòu, nǐ hé fùmǔ huì yīqǐ zhù ma?
  Will you live together with your parents after you get married?
- 今天晚上老板要和我们 一起 加班。
  Jīntiān wǎnshang, lǎobǎn yào hé wǒmen yīqǐ jiābān.
  Tonight the boss is going to to work overtime together with us.

Similar to

- Expressing "with" with "gen" (HSK3)

Measure words for verbs

Also known as: 动量词 (dòng liàngcí), verbal measure word and verbal classifier.

When a verb is done more than once, it also requires a measure word to accompany it. This way the measure word is acting as a way to count the frequency or re-occurrence of an action. The most basic one you probably already know is 次 (cì).

Structure

 Verb + Number + Measure Word

The grammar pattern is very similar to English. For example, "看三次" and "saw three times" mirror each other in structure. In Chinese sentences, these measure words come after the verb. You should also know that, like nouns, some verbs have special measure words to go with them. The basic verbal measure word, however, is 次, as in the number of "times" something is done or happens.

Common verb measure words include 次 (cì), 遍 (biàn), and 下 (xià).

Examples

- 再说一 遍 。
  Zài shuō yī biàn .
  Say it again.
- 你能再读一 遍 吗?
  Nǐ néng zài dú yī biàn ma?
  Could you please read it again?
- 这个电影我看过两 遍 。
  Zhège diànyǐng wǒ kàn guo liǎng biàn .
  I've seen this movie twice.
- 这个故事我听她说过一百多 遍 了。
  Zhège gùshi wǒ tīng tā shuō guo yī bǎi duō biàn le.
  I've heard her tell this story more than one hundred times.

- 我们去过两 次 。
  Wǒme qù guo liǎng cì.
  We've been there twice.
- 我问了他很多 次 ，可是他不告诉我。
  Wǒ wèn le tā hěn duō cì, kěshì tā bù gàosu wǒ.
  I've asked him about it many times, but he won't tell me.
- 这个问题我们讨论过几 次 。
  Zhège wèntí wǒmen tǎolùn guo jǐ cì.
  We've discussed this issue a few times.
- 那个红头发的男孩打了我三 下 。
  Nàge hóng tóufa de nánhái dǎ le wǒ sān xià.
  That red-haired boy hit me three times.
- 他轻轻地拍了我两 下 。
  Tā qīngqīng de pāi le wǒ liǎng xià.
  He very lightly pat me a few times.
- 你没听见吗？我敲了好几 下 。
  Nǐ méi tīngjiàn ma? Wǒ qiāo le hǎo jǐ xià.
  Did you not hear the door? I knocked quite a few times.

Similar to

- Measure words in quantity questions (HSK1)
- Expressing “every” with “mei” (HSK2), page 158
- Measure words for counting (HSK2), page 160
- Measure words with “this” and “that” (HSK2), page 163

Negative commands with "buyao"

You can use 不要 (bùyào) to command someone: "don't" (do something). This is similar to the other negative command "别 (bié)[1]."

Note: The pinyin for 不要 is written "bùyào" but pronounced "búyào" due to a tone change rule.

Structure

Negative commands in Chinese ("do not" or "don't") are formed with 不要. Usually the subject is omitted, as in English.

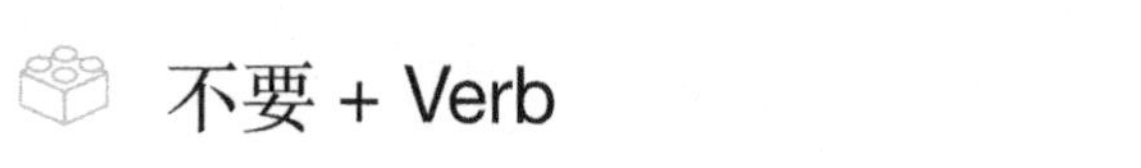

Examples

- 不要 走。
  Bùyào zǒu.
  Don't leave.
- 不要 打我！
  Bùyào dǎ wǒ!
  Don't hit me!
- 不要 生气，好吗?
  Bùyào shēngqì, hǎo ma?
  Don't get angry, OK?
- 不要 哭！
  Bùyào kū!
  Don't cry!
- 不要 吃很多肉。
  Bùyào chī hěn duō ròu.
  Don't eat a lot of meat.

---

1. Negative commands with "bie" (Grammar), page 34

- 你们 不要 喝酒。
  Nǐmen bùyào hējiǔ.
  You guys, don't drink alcohol.
- 不要 说英文。
  Bùyào shuō Yīngwén.
  Don't speak English.
- 晚上 不要 喝咖啡。
  Wǎnshang bùyào hē kāfēi.
  Don't drink coffee at night.
- 上课的时候 不要 玩手机！
  Shàngkè de shíhou bùyào wán shǒujī!
  In class don't play with your phone!
- 不要 很晚睡觉！
  Bùyào hěn wǎn shuìjiào.
  Don't go to bed too late.

Similar to

- Auxiliary verb "yao" and its multiple meanings (HSK2), page 102
- Negative commands with "bie" (HSK2), page 34
- Expressing "don't need to" with "buyong" (HSK4)

Reduplication of verbs

One of the fun things about Chinese is that when speaking, you can repeat a verb to express “a little bit” or “briefly.” This is called reduplication. It creates a casual tone, and a sense that whatever the action is, it’s not going to take long.

Reduplication with the AA Pattern

Structure

In Chinese, verbs can be reduplicated to indicate that they happen briefly or “a little bit.”

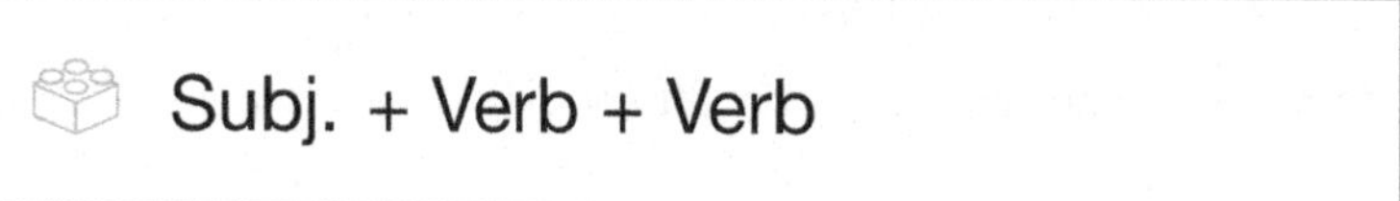

Chinese grammar books frequently refer to the reduplication of a single-character word as a “AA” pattern. Note that for this pattern, the second verb’s tone changes to the neutral tone.

Examples

- 你看看。
  Nǐ kànkan.
  Take a little look.
- 我试试。
  Wǒ shìshi.
  I'll give it a try.
- 说说你的想法。
  Shuōshuo nǐ de xiǎngfǎ.
  Talk a little bit about your ideas.
- 出去玩玩吧！
  Chūqù wánwan ba!
  Go out and have fun!
- 我想出去走走。
  Wǒ xiǎng chūqù zǒuzou.
  I want to go out and walk for a bit.

Reduplication with 一 (yī)

Structure

Another way to reduplicate verbs is to insert 一 (yī), in the following structure:

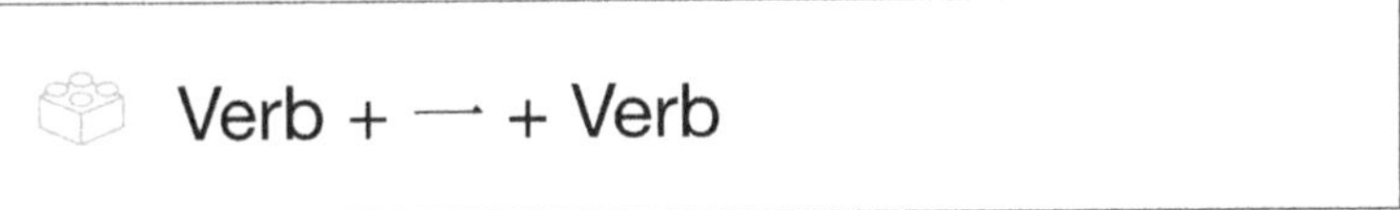

Examples

- 别生气了，笑一笑！
  Bié shēngqì le, xiào yī xiào!
  Don't be mad, gimme a smile!
- 你去问一问他们厕所在哪里。
  Nǐ qù wèn yī wèn tāmen cèsuǒ zài nǎlǐ.
  Go and ask them where the bathroom is.
- 我可以用一用你的电脑吗？
  Wǒ kěyǐ yòng yī yòng nǐ de diànnǎo ma?
  Can I use your computer for a little bit?
- 你现在有时间吗？我们聊一聊吧。
  Nǐ xiànzài yǒu shíjiān ma? Wǒmen liáo yī liáo ba.
  Do you have a second? Let's chat for a bit.
- 你想尝一尝我做的菜吗？
  Nǐ xiǎng cháng yī cháng wǒ zuò de cài ma?
  Do you want to taste the food that I cooked?

Using this kind of structure lightens the mood and seriousness of the question. It also adds variety to sentence structure. Because these phrases are used colloquially, there is not set rule to which verbs this can be applied to. There are some verbs that are often reduplicated and some verbs that sound weird when reduplicated. With practice and exposure, you will learn which ones are often used.

ABAB Reduplication with Two-Syllable Verbs

In the examples above, all verbs are only one syllable. Those verbs get reduplicated a lot, so those examples are quite useful. Occasionally, though, two-syllable verbs get reduplicated as well. When this happens, it's important to use the "ABAB" pattern for verbs (meaning the entire word is repeated), and not the "AABB" pattern you use for adjectives (where each character is repeated individually).

Examples

- 考虑考虑
  kǎolǜ kǎolǜ
  think it over
- 讨论讨论
  tǎolùn tǎolùn
  discuss it
- 商量商量
  shāngliang shāngliang
  talk it over
- 打听打听
  dǎting dǎting
  inquire about it

Similar to

- Softening speech with "ba" (HSK1)
- Reduplication of measure words (HSK2), page 59
- Verbing briefly with "yixia" (HSK2), page 131
- Reduplication of adjectives (HSK3)

Special cases of "zai" following verbs

When used to indicate locations of actions, 在 (zài) is usually placed after the subject and before the verb. There are certain cases, however, when 在 (zài) goes after the verb.

Structure

This pattern is used regularly with special types of verbs, including: 住 (zhù), 放 (fàng), 坐 (zuò), and 站 (zhàn). These are verbs that imply movement or location. Technically, the structure is called a location complement, but it can be understood without going into that much detail. Just remember that for verbs implying *movement* or *location* like the ones above, the default sentence order changes and you get this structure:

Subj. + [Special Verb] + 在 + Location

Examples

- 你住 在 上海 吗?
  Nǐ zhù zài Shànghǎi ma?
  Do you live in Shanghai?
- 他坐 在 老板的旁边 。
  Tā zuò zài lǎobǎn de pángbiān .
  He sits next to the boss.
- 你应该站 在 我后面 。
  Nǐ yīnggāi zhàn zài wǒ hòumiàn .
  You should stand behind me.
- 不要坐 在 我的床上 。
  Bùyào zuò zài wǒ de chuáng shàng .
  Don't sit on my bed.
- 你的衣服不可以放 在 这里 。
  Nǐ de yīfu bù kěyǐ fàng zài zhèlǐ .
  You can't put your clothes here.

- 不要站 在 路中间 。
  Bùyào zhàn zài lù zhōngjiān .
  Don't stand in the middle of the road.
- 不要坐 在 地上 。
  Bùyào zuò zài dì shàng .
  Don't sit on the ground.
- 那本书我放 在 桌子上 了。
  Nà běn shū wǒ fàng zài zhuōzi shàng le.
  I placed that book on the table.
- 不要走 在 草地上 。
  Búyào zǒu zài cǎodì shàng .
  Don't walk on the grass.
- 周末我不想待 在 家里 。
  Zhōumò wǒ bù xiǎng dāi zài jiā lǐ .
  I don't want to stay at home on weekends.

Remember that this is an *exception to the normal rule*. A common mistake is to over apply this and produce incorrect sentences. Note the incorrect and correct versions below.

✗ 我工作 在 上海。
Wǒ gōngzuò zài Shànghǎi.

✓ 我 在 上海工作。
Wǒ zài Shànghǎi gōngzuò.
I work in Shanghai.

✗ 我学习 在 图书馆。
Wǒ xuéxí zài túshūguǎn.

✓ 我 在 图书馆学习。
Wǒ zài túshūguǎn xuéxí.
I study in the library.

Similar to

- Expressing existence in a place with “zai” (HSK1)
- Indicating location with “zai” before verbs (HSK1)
- Expressing location with “zai... shang / xia / li” (HSK4)

Using "dao" to mean "to go to"

A simple and direct way to indicate that you or someone is going to a specific place or has arrived at a specific place is to use the verb 到 (dào).

到 (dào) for Arriving in a Place

Structure

The verb 到 (dào) is used to talk about arriving in places.

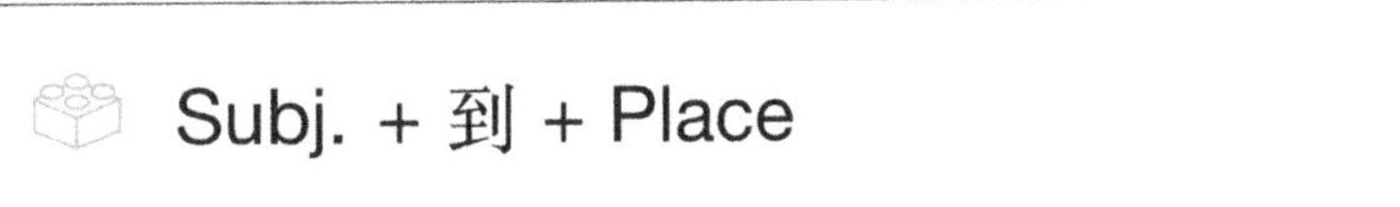
Subj. + 到 + Place

Examples

For these examples, it's straightforward to think of 到 (dào) as simply meaning "to arrive."

- 他们已经 到 酒吧了。
  Tāmen yǐjīng dào jiǔbā le.
  They have already arrived at the bar.
- 我刚 到 家。
  Wǒ gāng dào jiā.
  I just got home.
- 你 到 机场了吗?
  Nǐ dào jīchǎng le ma?
  Have you arrived at the airport?
- 我已经 到 火车站了。
  Wǒ yǐjīng dào huǒchēzhàn le.
  I've already arrived at the train station.
- 我们先 到 北京，然后 到 香港。
  Wǒmen xiān dào Běijīng, ránhòu dào Xiānggǎng.
  First we'll arrive in Beijing, then in Hong Kong.

In some examples translating 到 (dào) as "to arrive" doesn't work as well and you might need to expand your understanding of exactly what 到 (dào) means. That's what we'll examine below.

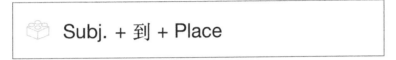

到 (dào) for Coming or Going to a Place

One commonly used structure takes the above one and adds a 来 (lái) or 去 (qù) to the end of the sentence.

Structure

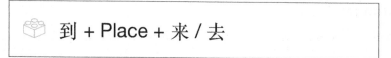

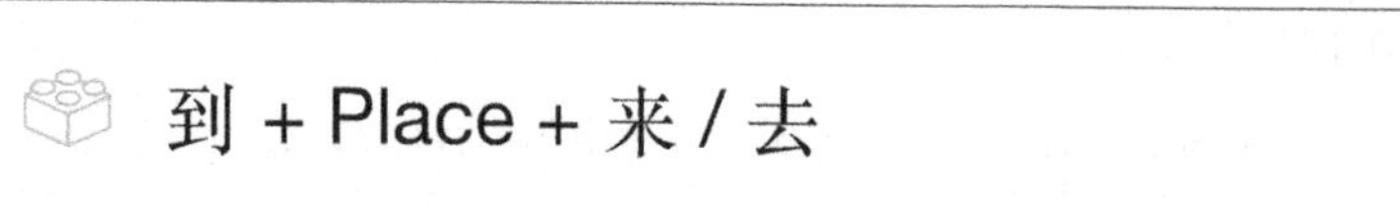

Examples

- 我下午在家，你可以 到 我家 来 。
  Wǒ xiàwǔ zài jiā, nǐ kěyǐ dào wǒ jiā lái.
  I'll be home this afternoon. You can come to my house.
- 老板马上 到 办公室 去 。
  Lǎobǎn mǎshàng dào bàngōngshì qù.
  The boss is going to the office right now.

Going to a Place and Performing an Action

Structure

If you are going to a place to do something else, you can first use 到 (dào) to indicate where you're going, then add another verb after that. This has the meaning of "going to the place to do something," and it's one case where the "arrive" translation doesn't really work anymore.

Examples

- 明天我要 到 南京路买衣服。
  Míngtiān wǒ yào dào Nánjīng Lù mǎi yīfu.
  Tomorrow I'll go to Nanjing Road to buy clothes.
- 你们晚上 到 哪儿吃饭啊?
  Nǐmen wǎnshang dào nǎr chīfàn a?
  Where will you all go to eat food this evening?

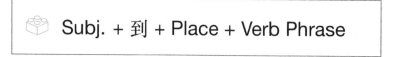

- 我跟朋友经常 到 KTV 唱歌。

  Wǒ gēn péngyou jīngcháng dào KTV chànggē.

  I often go to Karaoke to sing songs with friends.

- 今年春节我要 到 女朋友家见她的父母。

  Jīnnián Chūnjié wǒ yào dào nǚpéngyou jiā jiàn tā de fùmǔ.

  This Spring Festival I am going to my girlfriend's house to meet her parents.

- 下个月我要 到 美国出差。

  Xià gè yuè wǒ yào dào Měiguó chūchāi.

  Next month I need to go to the USA on a business trip.

You might be wondering: *can I just use 去 (qù) instead of 到 (dào)?* For sentences like this, *yes, you can.* But native speakers will frequently use 到 (dào) in this way, so it's still good to be familiar with this pattern. If you want to sound more native, you should use it too!

到 (dào), 去 (qù), and 走 (zǒu)

Sometimes it can be hard to figure out exactly which word to use in Chinese to mean "go." 到 (dào) is used when you talk about *arriving* at a place, emphasizing the destination. 去 (qù) is used when you are *going to* a place. The exact meaning is "to go," and it emphasizes *getting to* somewhere. 走 (zǒu) is used when talking about "leaving." The emphasis is on getting *away* from a particular place.

Similar to

- Expressing "from· · · to· · ·" with "cong· · · dao· · ·" (HSK2), page 92

Using "hao" to mean "easy"

Of course 好 (hǎo) means "good." But it can also be used to express that something is "easy to do" or "good to do." And it is quite... *easy to do*! All you need to do is place a 好 (hǎo) before a verb.

General Verbs

Just as 难 (nán) can be used to indicate that it's hard to do something, 好 (hǎo) can also come before verbs to indicate that something is *easy to do*.

Structure

The simple form is just:

> 好 + Verb

If you want to make a sentence out of it:

> Subj. + (很) 好 + Verb

Examples

- 这个词的意思很 好懂 。
  Zhège cí de yìsi hěn hǎo dǒng .
  The meaning of this word is easy to understand.
- 这个汉字很 好写 。
  Zhège Hànzì hěn hǎo xiě .
  This Chinese character is easy to write.
- 三明治很 好做 。
  Sānmíngzhì hěn hǎo zuò .
  Sandwiches are easy to make.
- 苹果手机现在很 好买 。
  Píngguǒ shǒujī xiànzài hěn hǎo mǎi .
  iPhones are easy to buy now.

- 这个笔很 好用 。

  Zhège bǐ hěn hǎo yòng.

  This pen is easy to use.

Exceptions

好 (hǎo) can also be attached to "sense verbs" (e.g. "look," "taste," "smell," etc.) to indicate that something is **good *to do* (rather than "*easy* to do").**

There's a limited number of these, but some of them are super common, so just memorize them as exceptions:

- 好吃

  hǎochī

  good to taste, good to eat, delicious

- 好喝

  hǎohē

  good to taste, good to drink

- 好看

  hǎokàn

  good to look at, good-looking, attractive

- 好听

  hǎotīng

  good to listen to, pleasant to listen to, good-sounding

- 好闻

  hǎowén

  good to smell, smells good, good-smelling

The word for "fun" in Chinese is also of this form, even though it's not a sense verb:

- 好玩

  hǎowán

  fun

Examples

- 这首歌很 好听 。

  Zhè shǒu gē hěn hǎotīng.

  This song is great.

- 这种茶很 好闻 。
  Zhè zhǒng chá hěn hǎowén.
  This kind of tea smells good.
- 你的新包很 好看 。
  Nǐ de xīn bāo hěn hǎokàn.
  Your new bag looks good.
- 妈妈做的菜很 好吃 。
  Māma zuò de cài hěn hǎochī.
  The food mom makes is delicious.
- 我觉得上海很 好玩 。
  Wǒ juéde Shànghǎi hěn hǎowán.
  I think Shanghai is a lot of fun.

Similar to

- Expressing "difficult" with "nan" (HSK3)
- Expressing difficulty with "hao (bu) rongyi" (HSK5)
- Expressing purpose with "hao" (HSK5)

Verbing briefly with "yixia"

After briefly reading this article, you will know how to use 一下 (yīxià) to express a brief action!

Note: The pinyin for 一下 is written "yīxià" but pronounced "yíxià" due to a tone change rule.

Structure

To express that a verb is carried out briefly or "a little bit," you can add 一下 (yīxià) after it. Sometimes 一下 (yīxià) can soften the tone.

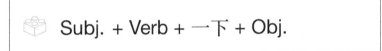

Subj. + Verb + 一下 + Obj.

Often, adding 一下 (yīxià) just makes the Chinese feel more natural. This is not something you can get a feel for quickly. You'll want to observe how native speakers use 一下 (yīxià) over a long period of time to really get used to how it is used.

Examples

- 请你等 一下 。
  Qǐng nǐ děng yīxià .
  Please wait a little bit.
  You get the feeling that it shouldn't be a long wait.
- 你看 一下 。
  Nǐ kàn yīxià .
  Take a look.
  It should be quick.
- 试 一下 吧。
  Shì yīxià ba.
  Try it.
  How long can trying it take?
- 我要想 一下 。
  Wǒ yào xiǎng yīxià .
  I want to think a little.
  You're supposed to believe that I won't need to think about it long.
- 开 一下 门吧。
  Kāi yīxià mén ba.
  Please open the door.
  How long can it take to open the door?

- 请你说 [一下] 为什么。
  Qǐng nǐ shuō [yīxià] wèishénme.
  Please say why.
  I feel it should be a quick explanation.
- 不要生气了，笑 [一下] ！
  Bùyào shēngqì le, xiào [yīxià]!
  Don't be mad, laugh!
  Just one quick laugh!
- 宝宝，亲 [一下] 爸爸。
  Bǎobao, qīn [yīxià] bàba.
  Baby, give your dad a kiss.
  If a baby's kiss isn't quick, it's weird for everyone.
- 你可以来 [一下] 我的办公室吗？
  Nǐ kěyǐ lái [yīxià] wǒ de bàngōngshì ma?
  Could you please come to my office?
  Just come real quick.
- 你能介绍 [一下] 自己吗？
  Nǐ néng jièshào [yīxià] zìjǐ ma?
  Could you introduce yourself briefly?
  Not your life story, just a brief self-introduction.

Similar to

- Reduplication of verbs (HSK2, HSK3), page 120

Verbs followed by "gei"

Although it's standard practice to put a word or phrase that modifies a verb *before* the verb, there are, of course, exceptions. 给 (gěi) is one of those exceptions; it sometimes comes before the verb[1] and sometimes after. This article is about when it comes after.

Basic Pattern

Structure

Note that the verbs that fit into this pattern are normally single-syllable verbs.

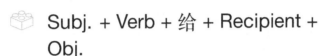

Subj. + Verb + 给 + Recipient + Obj.

or

Obj. + Subj. + Verb + 给 + Recipient

Examples

- 昨天有人 送给 我一束花。

  Zuótiān yǒu rén sòng gěi wǒ yī shù huā.

  Yesterday someone gave me a bouquet of flowers.

- 请 递给 我一盒纸巾。

  Qǐng dì gěi wǒ yī hé zhǐjīn.

  Please pass me a box of tissues.

- 这是我们 送给 你的生日礼物。

  Zhè shì wǒmen sòng gěi nǐ de shēngrì lǐwù.

  This is your birthday present from us.

1. Verbs preceded by "gei" (Grammar), page 136

- 这本书是谁 借给 你的?
  Zhè běn shū shì shéi jiè gěi nǐ de?
  Who lent you this book?
- 邮件我已经 发给 你了。
  Yóujiàn wǒ yǐjīng fā gěi nǐ le.
  I sent you that email already.

Advanced Pattern

Structure

Additionally, you can add 把 into this structure. This does not change the meaning of the sentence and when used in context can even add emphasis to what's being done and given.

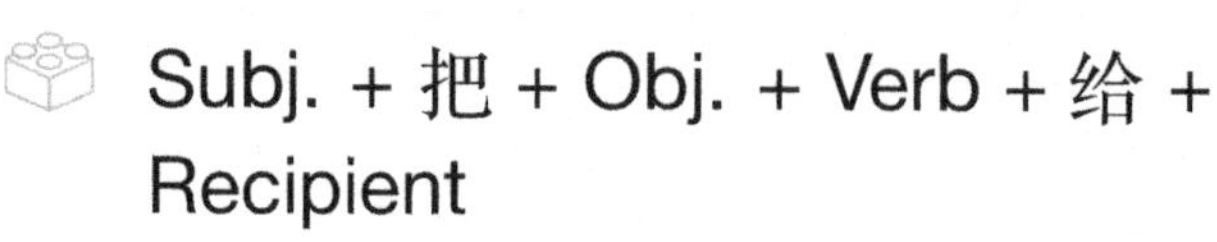

Subj. + 把 + Obj. + Verb + 给 + Recipient

Examples

- 你想 把 这个礼物 送给 谁?
  Nǐ xiǎng bǎ zhège lǐwù sòng gěi shéi?
  Who are you going to give this present to?
- 请 把 那些照片都 发给 我。
  Qǐng bǎ nàxiē zhàopiàn dōu fā gěi wǒ.
  Please send all of those pictures to me.
- 我已经 把 车 卖给 了一个朋友。
  Wǒ yǐjīng bǎ chē mài gěi le yī gè péngyou.
  I've already sold my car to a friend of mine.
- 请 把 盐 递给 我，谢谢。
  Qǐng bǎ yán dì gěi wǒ, xièxie.
  Please pass me the salt. Thanks.
- 可以 把 这本书 借给 我吗?
  Kěyǐ bǎ zhè běn shū jiè gěi wǒ ma?
  Could you please lend me this book?

Note that the verb 嫁 (jià) cannot fit into the 把 pattern above; it's an exception.

- 她 嫁给 了一个有钱的老头。

  Tā jià gěi le yī gè yǒuqián de lǎotóu.

  She married a rich old man.

If you really want to make a 把 sentence, though, you can do it in this sexist way:

- 她爸爸 把 她 嫁给 了一个有钱的老头。

  Tā bàba bǎ tā jià gěi le yī gè yǒuqián de lǎotóu.

  Her father married her off to a rich old man.

Academic Debate

Although 给 phrases should normally precede a verb like any other prepositional phrase, they sometimes come after. Why have it both ways? There is some academic debate over whether this 给 is actually a preposition, a type of verb (often called a "co-verb"), or even a type of complement. This type of discussion is outside the scope of this article, however.

Similar to

- Expressing "for" with "gei" (HSK2), page 90
- Using "dui" with verbs (HSK2), page 97
- Verbs preceded by "gei" (HSK2), page 136

Verbs preceded by “gei”

The word 给 (gěi) literally means “to give” but is frequently used in Chinese to indicate the *target* of a verb. The target is who or what the verb is aimed or directed at.

Structure

Examples

- 现在不要 给 他 打电话 。
  Xiànzài bùyào gěi tā dǎ diànhuà .
  Don't give him a phone call now.
- 请快点 给 我 回邮件 。
  Qǐng kuàidiǎn gěi wǒ huí yóujiàn .
  Please hurry up and reply to my email.
- 他说他会 给 我 写信 的。
  Tā shuō tā huì gěi wǒ xiě xìn de.
  He said he would write letters to me.
- 你可以 给 大家 读一下 吗?
  Nǐ kěyǐ gěi dàjiā dú yīxià ma?
  Could you please read it for everybody?
- 我 给 你 发短信 了，你怎么不回?
  Wǒ gěi nǐ fā duǎnxìn le. Nǐ zěnme bù huí?
  I sent you a text. Why didn't you reply?
- 她的粉丝常常 给 她 寄礼物 。
  Tā de fěnsī chángcháng gěi tā jì lǐwù .
  Her fans often send her gifts.

- 小时候，妈妈每天都 给 我 讲故事 。
  Xiǎo shíhou, māma měi tiān dōu gěi wǒ jiǎng gùshi .
  When I was young, my mother would tell me stories every day.
- 爸爸应该 给 儿子 道歉 。
  Bàba yīnggāi gěi érzi dàoqiàn .
  The father should apologize to his son.
- 谁能 给 我 解释一下 ？
  Shéi néng gěi wǒ jiěshì yīxià ?
  Who can explain this to me?
- 老板让我明天 给 客户 介绍我们的新产品 。
  Lǎobǎn ràng wǒ míngtiān gěi kèhù jièshào wǒmen de xīn chǎnpǐn .
  My boss asked to present our new product to the client tomorrow.

Chinese speakers use 给 in some interesting ways, similar to how English speakers use "to give," as in "to give someone a phone call" or "to give someone a reply."

Alternative Structure

Although the structure above is the best one to learn first, some verbs frequently use 给 but have the 给 coming after the verb, rather than before. It's best to think of these as exceptions to the rule above, and you can learn more about these exceptions by reading about verbs followed by "gei"[1].

Similar to

- Expressing "for" with "gei" (HSK2), page 90
- Using "dui" with verbs (HSK2), page 97
- Verbs followed by "gei" (HSK2), page 133
- Verbs that take double objects (HSK2), page 138
- Expressing "until" with "dao" (HSK4)

---

1. Verbs followed by "gei" (Grammar), page 133

Verbs that take double objects

There are some common verbs in Chinese that can take two objects. In this article, we will look at how they are used.

Structure

As in English, some verbs in Chinese take two objects. A typical example for English is "to bake someone a cake," and there are countless more. The structure in Chinese is:

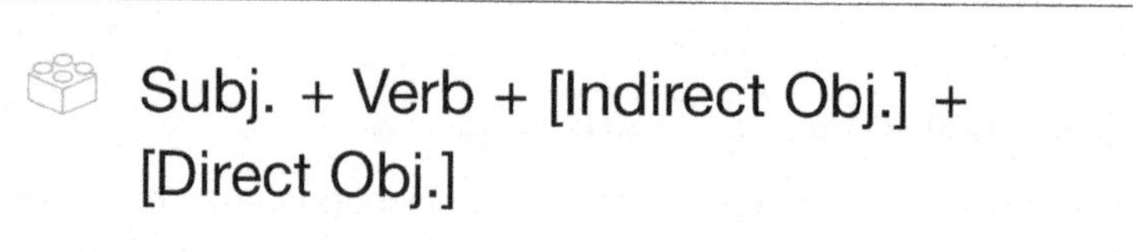

If you don't know what direct and indirect objects are, don't worry; the terms can be thought of as "object 1" and "object 2." The main point is that there are two of them, and the first one is the recipient (e.g. the person the cake is given to), while the second one is the thing that the action happens to (e.g. the cake that gets baked).

Examples

- 老师，我可以 问 你 一个 问题 吗？
  Lǎoshī, wǒ kěyǐ wèn nǐ yī gè wèntí ma?
  Teacher, may I ask you a question?
- 大家都 叫 他 "怪叔叔"。
  Dàjiā dōu jiào tā "guài shūshu."
  Everyone calls him "Uncle Weirdo."
- 我想 告诉 你 一个好 消息。
  Wǒ xiǎng gàosu nǐ yī gè hǎo xiāoxi.
  I want to tell you the good news.
- 他们 给 了 你 多少钱？
  Tāmen gěi le nǐ duōshao qián?
  How much money did they give you?
- 他 送 了 女朋友 很多 花。
  Tā sòng le nǚpéngyou hěn duō huā.
  He gave his girlfriend lots of flowers.

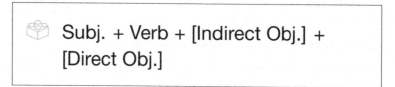

- 我想 送给 你 一本 书 。
  Wǒ xiǎng sòng gěi nǐ yī běn shū .
  I want to give you a book.
- 爸爸要 送给 我 一个很贵的 生日礼物 。
  Bàba yào sòng gěi wǒ yī gè hěn guì de shēngrì lǐwù .
  My dad is going to give me a very expensive birthday gift.
- 你可以 借 我 两千块钱 吗?
  Nǐ kěyǐ jiè wǒ liǎng qiān kuài qián ma?
  Can you lend me 2000 kuai?
- 老板刚 发给 我 上个月的 工资 。
  Lǎobǎn gāng fā gěi wǒ shàng gè yuè de gōngzī .
  The boss just gave me my pay for last month.
- 这个人 骗 了 我 很多 钱 。
  Zhège rén piàn le wǒ hěn duō qián .
  This person cheated me out of a lot of money.

Similar to

- Verbs preceded by "gei" (HSK2), page 136

Degree complement

Also known as: 程度补语 (chéngdù bǔyǔ) and complement of degree.

While most complements follow verbs, degree complements can follow both verbs and adjectives. These complements intensify or modify the degree of expression of the verb or adjective.

When to use it

Until now, you may have been getting by just fine modifying your verbs with adverbs. You can use 非常 to say "very" and all that. Great. But once you learn to use degree complements, a whole new layer of expressiveness is infused into your language. You will be able to express **degree** of verbs and adjectives with much more precision and color. But how do you know *when to use* the degree complement? Here are the main reasons to use it:

1. To express **how** a verb happened or assess its quality
2. To express **to what extent** (or degree) an adjective is true

For the first case, the most typical examples would be describing *how well* an action is done, or in *asking* how well an action is done, which are sometimes also classified as descriptive complements and state complements.

- 你们觉得我画 得怎么样 ？
  Nǐmen juéde wǒ huà de zěnmeyàng? — *The complement is used to ask "how well I draw."*
- 我们觉得你画 得很好 。
  Wǒmen juéde nǐ huà de hěn hǎo. — *The complement tells us that "you draw very well."*
- 他英语说 得怎么样 ？
  Tā Yīngyǔ shuō de zěnmeyàng? — *The complement is used to ask "how well he speaks English."*
- 他英语说 得一般 。
  Tā Yīngyǔ shuō de yībān. — *The complement tells us that "His English is average."*

Basic Pattern Following Verbs

We can use all kinds of degree complements to add some color to our verbs.

Structure

Examples

- 你做 得不错 。

  Nǐ zuò de bùcuò.

  You're doing a great job.

- 孩子们学 得挺快的 。

  Háizi men xué de tǐng kuài de.

  The kids are learning fast.

- 我吃 得太饱了 。

  Wǒ chī de tài bǎo le.

  I'm stuffed.

- 你们谈 得顺利 吗?

  Nǐmen tán de shùnlì ma?

  Did your conversation go well?

- 她长 得还可以 。

  Tā zhǎng de hái kěyǐ.

  She is all right-looking.

Degree Complements with Objects

Both adding a complement to a verb with an object and adding an objective to a verb with a complement complicate a sentence in Mandarin, because *a single verb cannot be followed by both an object and a complement*. In order to get all three pieces of information into a grammatically correct Chinese sentence, there are two approaches to take:

Approach #1: Repeat the Verb

✔ 你 说 中文 说 得很好 。

Nǐ shuō Zhōngwén shuō de hěn hǎo.

You speak Chinese well. (lit. You speak Chinese speak it well.)

Just like little kids, objects and complements don't know how to share. Make sure each gets its own (identical) verb. Also make sure that the object comes after the first instance of the verb, and the complement after the second.

Approach #2: Move the Object to the Front

✔ 你的 中文 说 得很好 。

Nǐ de Zhōngwén shuō de hěn hǎo.

You speak Chinese well. (lit. You Chinese speak well.)

Note: the 你的中文 in the sentence above can also be 你中文 (without the 的). When it makes sense to include the 的, it often sounds better.

Just to be completely clear, the following sentences are both *incorrect*:

✗ 你 说 中文 很好 。
Nǐ shuō Zhōngwén hěn hǎo.

✗ 你 说 中文 得很好 。
Nǐ shuō Zhōngwén de hěn hǎo.

A few more examples:

- 你 做 菜 做 得很好 。
  Nǐ zuò cài zuò de hěn hǎo.
  You cook very well.
- 你的 菜 做 得很好 。
  Nǐ de cài zuò de hěn hǎo.
  You cook very well.
- 你 写 字 写 得很漂亮 。
  Nǐ xiě zì xiě de hěn piàoliang.
  Your handwriting is beautiful.
- 你的 字 写 得很漂亮 。
  Nǐ de zì xiě de hěn piàoliang.
  Your handwriting is beautiful.

Degree Complements Following Adjectives

Common Patterns

There are three especially common degree complements which can follow adjectives immediately and are *not* preceded by a 得:

- 极了 often comes after adjectives with positive connotations (often 好), indicating an extremely high degree.
- 死了 usually comes after adjectives with negative connotations (like 忙, 累, 臭, 难看) and are commonly used to exaggerate the degree of how bad something is. In recent years, however, 死了 also comes after adjectives with positive connotations.
- 坏了 is a bit like the complement 死了 and can be used to mean "extremely" in either a positive or a negative sense.

Examples

- 味道 好 极了。

  Wèidào hǎo jíle.

  The taste is amazing.

- 这里的天气 舒服 极了。

  Zhèlǐ de tiānqì shūfu jíle.

  The weather here is so comfortable.

- 他的袜子 臭 死了。

  Tā de wàzi chòu sǐle.

  His socks totally reek.

- 小狗 可爱 死了。

  Xiǎogǒu kě'ài sǐle.

  The puppy is so adorable!

- 老师说今天没有作业，我们都 高兴 坏了。

  Lǎoshī shuō jīntiān méiyǒu zuòyè, wǒmen dōu gāoxìng huàile.

  The teacher said there's no homework for today, which thrilled us all.

- 找不到孩子，妈妈 急 坏了。

  Zhǎo bu dào háizi, māma jí huàile.

  Having not found the child, the mother was an anxious wreck.

Note that 死 can also act as a result complement in verb phrases such as 打死 (literally, "beat to death"). In the examples above, however, it merely indicates an extreme degree (no actual deaths involved!).

Compared with Potential Complements

Some sentences that contain adjective complements may be indistinguishable as degree or potential complements when they are taken out of context. The following table explains different meanings that one complement phrase could have as either a degree complement or potential complement.

- 她说得清楚

  tā shuō de qīngchu

  she speaks clearly (Degree Complement Translation)

  she is able to speak clearly (Potential Complement Translation)

- 他们做得好

  tāmen zuò de hǎo

  they do it well (Degree Complement Translation)

  they are able to do it well (Potential Complement Translation)

- 他跑得快

  tā pǎo de kuài

  he runs fast (Degree Complement Translation)

  he is able to run fast (Potential Complement Translation)

Degree complements are commonly directly preceded by an adverb like 很. For example: 她说得很清楚. This serves to distinguish them from potential complements, which are never directly preceded by an adverb.

Descriptive and State Complements

Not every aspect of Chinese grammar is agreed upon in the world of academia, and this is the case with degree complements, descriptive complements, and state complements. Some scholars hold that the three are distinct, while others posit they're all just types of degree complements. Still, others maintain that degree complements are one, and descriptive complements and state complements are also one.

Here's how a professor of Chinese at Yale puts it:

> *Generally speaking, the complement of degree is a grammatical unit that describes the main verb of the sentence. Specifically, the complement of degree is an assessment of an action or a description of the consequential state of an action. It may also be a description of the degree of a state.*

Okayyy, so it sounds like descriptions and states are all degree complements? That's one of the views on the issue.

None of these classifications truly matters though: the key is *understanding* them and *using* complements correctly to express yourself in Chinese. (This is already difficult without adding in unnecessary academic distinctions!)

Similar to

- Direction complement (HSK3, HSK4)
- Advanced degree complements (HSK5)

Potential complement "-bu dong" for not understanding

Chinese learners often have to express that they don't understand something, especially in the beginning when they start learning. One of the ways to express that is to use the 不懂 (bù dǒng) verb complement.

Structure

Yes, 不懂 (bù dǒng) by itself simply means "not understand," and you can use it this way. But you'll find that more often, it follows a verb. When used this way, it is a complement.

The potential complement 不懂 (bù dǒng) is used to talk about things that can't be understood. Note that this is about *potential*: the subject doesn't have the *ability* to understand.

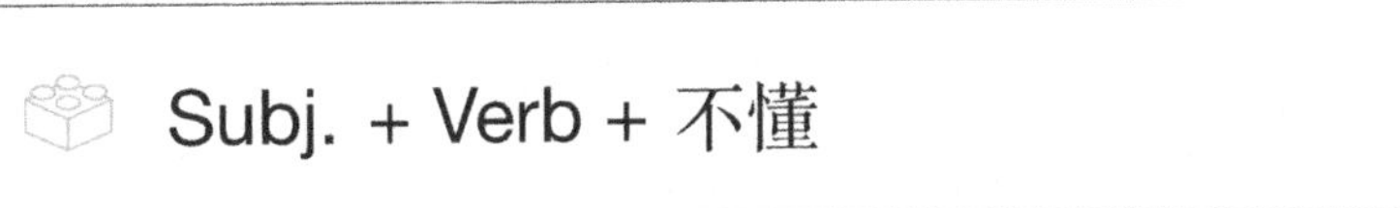

The 不懂 (bù dǒng) may also be swapped out with 不明白 (bù míngbai).

Examples

- 我 看 不懂 这本书。
  Wǒ kàn bu dǒng zhè běn shū.
  I don't understand the book.
  Literally, "read-not-understand"
- 孩子们 看 不懂 你写的汉字。
  Háizi men kàn bu dǒng nǐ xiě de Hànzì.
  Kids don't understand the characters that you wrote.
  Literally, "read-not-understand"
- 你 看 不懂 我的邮件吗?
  Nǐ kàn bu dǒng wǒ de yóujiàn ma?
  Do you not understand my emails?
  Literally, "read-not-understand"

- 老板的中文说得很好，可是他 看 不懂 中文报纸。
  Lǎobǎn de Zhōngwén shuō de hěn hǎo, kěshì tā kàn bu dǒng Zhōngwén bàozhǐ.
  The boss speaks very good Chinese, but he doesn't understand Chinese newspapers.
  Literally, "read-not-understand"
- 我 听 不懂 上海话。
  Wǒ tīng bu dǒng Shànghǎi-huà.
  I don't understand Shanghai dialect.
  Literally, "hear-not-understand"
- 你们 听 不懂 我的话吗?
  Nǐmen tīng bu dǒng wǒ de huà ma?
  Do you not understand what I say?
  Literally, "hear-not-understand"
- 我 听 不懂 你说的英语。
  Wǒ tīng bu dǒng nǐ shuō de Yīngyǔ.
  I don't understand your English.
  Literally, "hear-not-understand"
- 我们都 听 不懂 你的意思。
  Wǒmen dōu tīng bu dǒng nǐ de yìsi.
  None of us understand what you mean.
  Literally, "hear-not-understand"
- 很多人 读 不懂 这本书。
  Hěn duō rén dú bu dǒng zhè běn shū.
  Many people don't understand this book.
  Literally, "read-not-understand"
- 这个句子很难，学生们都 读 不懂 。
  Zhège jùzi hěn nán, xuéshengmen dōu dú bu dǒng.
  This sentence is very difficult. None of the students understand.
  Literally, "read-not-understand"

Similar to

- Result complements (HSK2, HSK3), page 150
- Advanced result complements (HSK5)

Result complement "-wan" for finishing

On its own, 完 (wán) means "to finish" or "to complete." Using it in this grammar structure, it expresses the idea of doing some action to completion.

Basic Usage

Structure

As well as with 到 (dào) and 见 (jiàn)[1], you can also form result complements with 完 (wán). This indicates that an action is finished or completed.

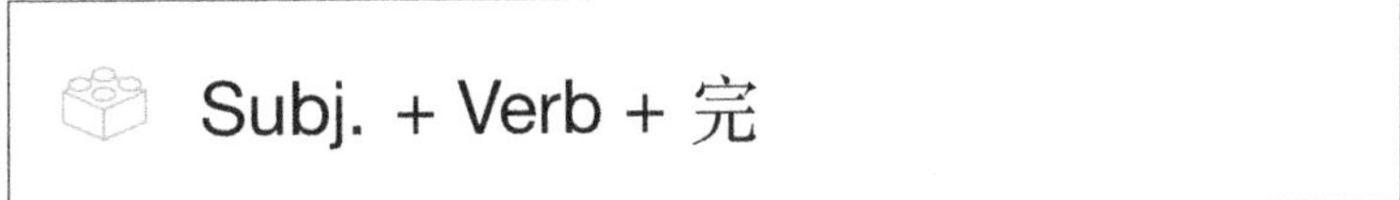

Examples

- 我们明天可以做 完 。
  Wǒmen míngtiān kěyǐ zuò wán .
  We can finish doing it tomorrow.
- 你能吃 完 吗?
  Nǐ néng chī wán ma?
  Can you finish eating all?
- 我今天要写 完 。
  Wǒ jīntiān yào xiě wán .
  I need to finish writing it today.
- 我没看 完 。
  Wǒ méi kàn wán .
  I didn't finish reading it.

Usage of 完了 (wán le)

Frequently, you'll also see a 了 (le) at the end, indicating completion.

---

1. Result complements "-dao" and "-jian" (Grammar), page 155

Structure

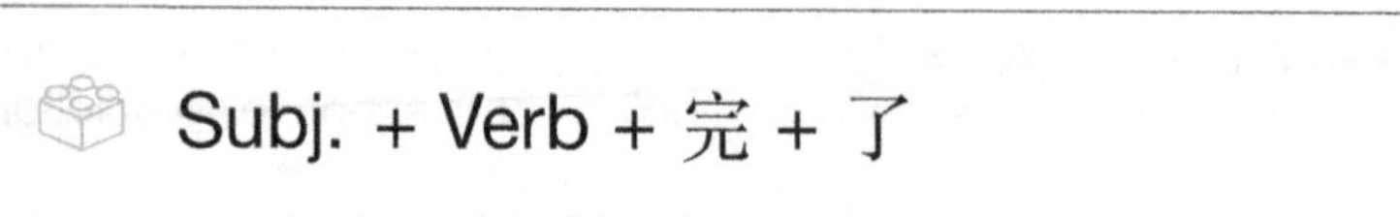

Examples

- 我说 完 了 。
  Wǒ shuō wán le .
  I am finished talking.
- 你吃 完 了 吗?
  Nǐ chī wán le ma?
  Are you done eating?
- 我看 完 了。
  Wǒ kàn wán le .
  I have finished watching it.
- 卖 完 了 。
  Mài wán le .
  It's sold out.
- 我们打扫 完 了 。
  Wǒmen dǎsǎo wán le .
  We finished cleaning.

Where to put the object

If there is an object followed by the verb, 完 must be placed between the verb and the object. To indicate completion, 了 usually goes after the object.

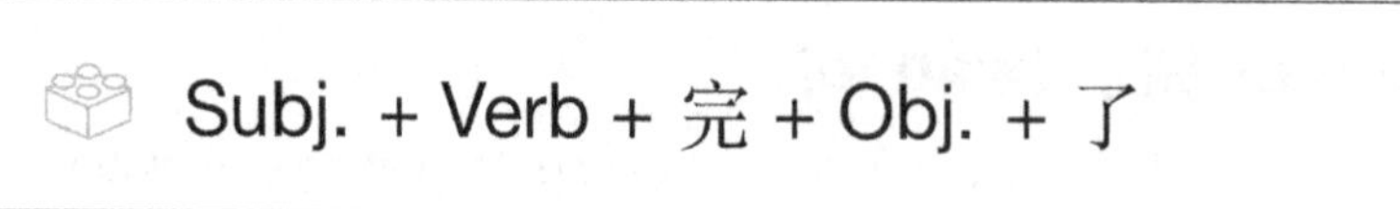

A few examples:

- 我做 完 作业 了 。
  Wǒ zuò wán zuòyè le.
  I finished doing my homework.

- 老板开 完 会 了 。
  Lǎobǎn kāi wán huì le.
  The boss finished having the meeting.
- 我看 完 这本书 了 。
  Wǒ kàn wán zhè běn shū le.
  I finished reading this book.
- 我们学 完 这篇课文 了 。
  Wǒmen xué wán zhè piān kèwén le.
  We finished studying this lesson.

In English we say "I finished the movie," or "I finished supper," but in Chinese you should explicitly use the verb implied in English along with 完了 (wán le) to emphasize that you completed the action: "watch the movie (till the end)" or "eat (all my) supper."

✘ 我 完 了电影。
Wǒ wán le diànyǐng.

✔ 我看 完 了电影。
Wǒ kàn wán le diànyǐng.
I finished watching the movie.

To tell us that you watched it till the end.

Similar to

- Result complements (HSK2, HSK3), page 150
- Result complements "-dao" and "-jian" (HSK2), page 155
- Advanced potential complements (HSK5)
- Advanced result complements (HSK5)

Result complements

Result complements come immediately after verbs to indicate that an action has led to a certain result and make that result clear to the listener. Often the complement is simply an adjective like 好 (hǎo) or a single syllable like 完 (wán).

Using Adjectives

好 (hǎo) implies that something is done to *completion* or done *well*. Forming a result complement with 好 has a very similar meaning to forming one with 完. It expresses that the action has been completed successfully.

错 (cuò) is used to express that an action has been performed incorrectly in some way, resulting in a mistake (错). This pattern covers what is often expressed with the adverb "incorrectly" in English.

Other adjectives commonly used as result complements include: 晚 (wǎn), 饱 (bǎo), 坏 (huài), 清楚 (qīngchu), 干净 (gānjìng), 破 (pò).

Structure

For the basic structure, you'll almost always see a 了 after the complement:

Subj. + Verb + Adj. + 了 (+ Obj.)

To negate a result complement, use 没 instead of 不:

Subj. + 没 + Verb + Adj. (+ Obj.)

Examples

- 你吃好了吗?
  Nǐ chī hǎo le ma?
  Are you done eating?
- 对不起，我记错了时间。
  Duìbuqǐ, wǒ jì cuò le shíjiān.
  Sorry, I misremembered the time.

- 你来 晚 了 ，我们已经关门 了 。
  Nǐ lái wǎn le , wǒmen yǐjīng guānmén le .
  You came too late. We're already closed.
- 他玩 坏 了 哥哥的玩具。
  Tā wán huài le gēge de wánjù.
  He broke his older brother's toy.
- 我 没 吃 饱 。
  Wǒ méi chī bǎo.
  I didn't get full.
- 他还 没 想 好 。
  Tā hái méi xiǎng hǎo.
  He hasn't thought it through yet.
- 我们 没 听 清楚 ，请再说一遍。
  Wǒmen méi tīng qīngchu, qǐng zài shuō yī biàn.
  We didn't hear it clearly. Please say it again.

When using result complements, it's very common to make the object a topic. This means the object is moved to the beginning of the sentence and the subject is often omitted.

Some examples:

- 这个字 写 错 了。
  Zhège zì xiě cuò le.
  You wrote this character wrong.
- 杯子 摔 坏 了。
  Bēizi shuāi huài le.
  The cup is broken.
- 房间 打扫 干净 了吗?
  Fángjiān dǎsǎo gānjìng le ma?
  Is your room all cleaned up?

Using One-Syllable Verbs

Besides adjectives, there are a few single-syllable verbs which can also be used as result complements. Some examples include 到 (dào), 见 (jiàn)[1], 懂

1. Result complements "-dao" and "-jian" (Grammar), page 155

(dǒng), 会 (huì), 走 (zǒu), 掉 (diào). There really aren't a lot of these, which is part of the reason why these are usually seen as one verb instead of a verb-complement structure.

Structure

For the basic structure, you'll often see a 了 after the complement:

> Subj. + Verb + [One-syllable Verb] + 了 (+ Obj.)

Examples

- 你们都 听懂 了吗?
  Nǐmen dōu tīng dǒng le ma?
  Do you all understand?
- 我看了，但是没 看懂 。
  Wǒ kàn le, dànshì méi kàn dǒng.
  I read it, but I didn't really understand it.
- 你 踩到 了我的脚。
  Nǐ cǎi dào le wǒ de jiǎo.
  You're stepping on my foot.
- 我不小心 撞到 了墙。
  Wǒ bù xiǎoxīn zhuàng dào le qiáng.
  I hit the wall by accident.
- 我女儿 学会 了数数。
  Wǒ nǚ'ér xué huì le shǔ shù.
  My daughter has learned how to count.
- 我爸爸还没 学会 用智能手机。
  Wǒ bàba hái méi xué huì yòng zhìnéng shǒujī.
  My father hasn't learned how to use a smartphone yet.
- 老师 拿走 了我的 iPad 。
  Lǎoshī ná zǒu le wǒ de iPad.
  The teacher took away my iPad.

- 小偷 偷走 了我的钱包。
  Xiǎotōu tōu zǒu le wǒ de qiánbāo.
  The thief stole my wallet.
- 他不小心 推倒 了一个老人。
  Tā bù xiǎoxīn tuī dǎo le yī gè lǎorén.
  He pushed over an old person by accident.
- 你 撞倒 了我的自行车。
  Nǐ zhuàng dǎo le wǒ de zìxíngchē.
  You knocked over my bike.
- 谁 扔掉 了我的袜子?
  Shéi rēng diào le wǒ de wàzi?
  Who threw away my socks?
- 我 卖掉 了我的旧手机。
  Wǒ mài diào le wǒ de jiù shǒujī.
  I sold my old cell phone.

Compared with Potential Complements

Result Complement	Aff. Potential Complement	Neg. Potential Complement
做完	做 得 完	做 不 完
听懂	听 得 懂	听 不 懂
看清楚	看 得 清楚	看 不 清楚
洗干净	洗 得 干净	洗 不 干净

Used in 把 Sentences

Although we have avoided 把 sentences in this article for the sake of simplicity, you may have noticed that sentences which feature result complements often also use 把. This is because 把 sentences and result complements work particularly well together, as they both deal with the result of an action or the "disposal" of an object. Apart from result complements involving perception and psychological verbs, most result compounds work nicely in 把 sentences.

- 我 把 杯子 摔坏 了。
  Wǒ bǎ bēizi shuāi huài le .
  I broke the glass.
- 他 把 我的电脑 修好 了。
  Tā bǎ wǒ de diànnǎo xiū hǎo le .
  He fixed my computer.
- 小偷 把 我的钱包 偷走 了。
  Xiǎotōu bǎ wǒ de qiánbāo tōu zǒu le .
  The thief made off with my wallet.
- 我们 把 房间 打扫干净 了。
  Wǒmen bǎ fángjiān dǎsǎo gānjìng le .
  We've cleaned the room.

Similar to

- Result complement "-wan" for finishing (HSK2), page 147
- Using "bei" sentences (HSK3)
- Expressing "mistakenly think that" with "yiwei" (HSK4)
- Expressing not knowing how to do something using "hao" (HSK4)
- Adjectival complement "de hen" (HSK5)

Result complements "-dao" and "-jian"

Two of the most common result complements in Chinese are 到 (dào) and 见 (jiàn). On this page we're only going to be talking about verbs related to the senses ("see," "hear," etc.), and for this usage, the two are interchangeable.

Verbs with 到 (dào) and 见 (jiàn)

Structure

Result complements are a huge topic in Chinese grammar, but you can approach them in stages. The structure you come across the most is a verb with 到 (dào):

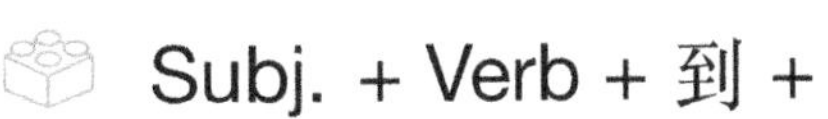

What 到 (dào) does is indicate that the outcome of the verb is achieved - what its *result* is. Without a result complement, the sentence would describe only the action itself. To illustrate, 看 (kàn) "to look" is the action of turning your head in a particular direction and focusing your eyes, whereas 看到 (kàndào), "to see," is the result of your brain taking in the visual input. It may sound a little hokey, but it really is possible to "look but not see," and Chinese makes a clear distinction between the action and the result.

The complement 见 (jiàn) is very similar to 到 (dào), and it is used in the same way:

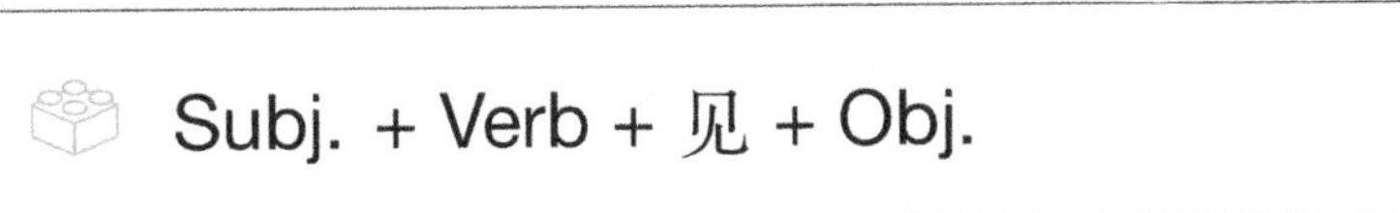

However, there is a difference. 见 (jiàn) is generally *only* used after verbs involving one of the senses, like 听 (tīng) and 看 (kàn), whereas 到 (dào) can be attached to a large variety of verbs, which we will discuss at a higher level later.

Examples

- 你 看 见 那个帅哥了吗?
  Nǐ kàn jiàn nàge shuàigē le ma?

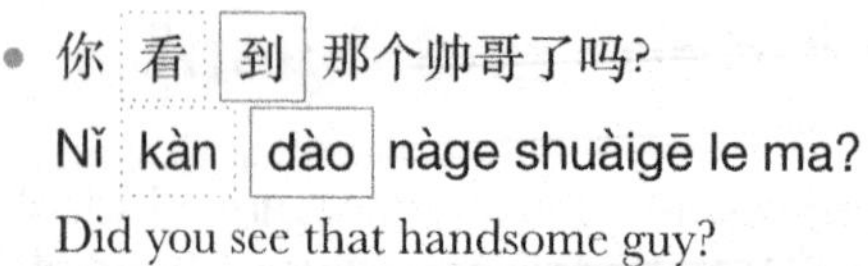

- 你 看 到 那个帅哥了吗？
  Nǐ kàn dào nàge shuàigē le ma?
  Did you see that handsome guy?
- 我 看 见 了。
  Wǒ kàn jiàn le.
- 我 看 到 了。
  Wǒ kàn dào le.
  I saw it.

We didn't say what "I" saw; you have to infer it from the context.

- 你 听 见 了吗？
  Nǐ tīng jiàn le ma?
- 你 听 到 了吗？
  Nǐ tīng dào le ma?
  Did you hear it?

Negative Forms

Structure

This structure can be negated using 没 (méi) on 没有 (méiyǒu). This is because if there is a result, then it already happened. And you need to use 没 (méi) to negate past events, not 不 (bù).

Examples

- 你 没 看 到 那个帅哥吗？
  Nǐ méi kàn dào nàge shuàigē ma?
- 你 没 看 见 那个帅哥吗？
  Nǐ méi kàn jiàn nàge shuàigē ma?
  You didn't see that handsome guy?
- 我 没有 看 到 。
  Wǒ méiyǒu kàn dào.

- 我 没有 看 见 。
  Wǒ méiyǒu kàn jiàn.
  I didn't see it.

We didn't say what "I" didn't see; you have to infer it from the context.

- 你 没 听 到 吗?
  Nǐ méi tīng dào ma?
- 你 没 听 见 吗?
  Nǐ méi tīng jiàn ma?
  You didn't hear it?

Similar to

- Result complement "-wan" for finishing (HSK2), page 147
- Result complements (HSK2, HSK3), page 150
- Advanced uses of direction complement "-qilai" (HSK4)
- Direction complement "-qilai" (HSK4)
- Advanced result complements (HSK5)
- Tricky uses of "dao" (HSK5)

Expressing "every" with "mei"

In this article we will look at the structure for saying "every" in Chinese, which is slightly more involved than just throwing in the word 每 (měi).

Structure

The pronoun 每 (měi) covers the meanings of "each" and "every." It should normally be used with a measure word and used with 都 (dōu)[1] in a complete sentence.

 每 + Measure Word + Noun + 都

Note that there are some words that don't use measure words because they themselves are already measure words. For example: 天 (tiān), 年 (nián), 周 (zhōu), 次 (cì) etc.

Examples

- 每个菜都好吃。
  Měi gè cài dōu hěn hǎochī.
  Every dish is delicious.
- 你每个人都认识吗?
  Nǐ měi gè rén dōu rènshi ma?
  Do you know every person?
- 老板每个月都出差。
  Lǎobǎn měi gè yuè dōu chūchāi.
  The boss goes on business trips every month.
- 他每天都不吃早饭。
  Tā měi tiān dōu bù chī zǎofàn.
  Every morning he skips breakfast.
- 他每年都来中国。
  Tā měi nián dōu lái Zhōngguó.
  He comes to China every year.

1. Emphasizing quantity with "dou" (Grammar), page 11

- 我 每 个星期 都 给妈妈打电话。
  Wǒ měi gè xīngqī dōu gěi māma dǎ diànhuà.
  I give mom a phone call every week.
- 这个班的 每 个学生 都 很聪明。
  Zhège bān de měi gè xuéshēng dōu hěn cōngming.
  Each of the students in this class are very smart.
- 老师 每 天 都 给我们很多作业。
  Lǎoshī měi tiān dōu gěi wǒmen hěn duō zuòyè.
  Every day the teacher gives us a lot of homework.
- 我们 每 周 都 要开会。
  Wǒmen měi zhōu dōu yào kāihuì.
  Every week we need to have a meeting.
- 他们 每 个周末 都 去公园。
  Tāmen měi gè zhōumò dōu qù gōngyuán.
  Every weekend they go to the park.

Similar to

- The "all" adverb "dou" (HSK1)
- Emphasizing quantity with "dou" (HSK2), page 11
- Expressing "every time" with "mei" and "dou" (HSK2), page 203
- Measure words for counting (HSK2), page 160
- Measure words for verbs (HSK2), page 116
- Expressing "as long as" with "fanshi" (HSK6)

Measure words for counting

Chinese uses measure words, a type of word called classifiers in linguistics which are common in East Asian languages. Measure words have a number of important uses, but one of the first ways you'll need to use them is for counting. Chinese learners should master them, starting with the measure word 个 (gè).

Structure

Whenever you talk about the quantity of something in Chinese, you need a measure word.

 Number + Measure Word + Noun

English does actually have measure words, it's just that most nouns usually don't need them. In English, most nouns are *count nouns* - they specify one instance of something. "An apple," for example. Some nouns are *mass nouns* and refer to something without specifying how much of it there is. Examples are "furniture," "paper," "water," etc. You can't say "a furniture"; you need a measure word: "a *piece* of furniture," "two *sheets* of paper," "three *glasses* of water," and so on.

In Chinese, *all* nouns are *mass nouns* so they all need measure words. Just as in English, different nouns are associated with different measure words (e.g. it wouldn't make sense to talk about "a glass of furniture" unless something went horribly wrong in the factory).

Examples

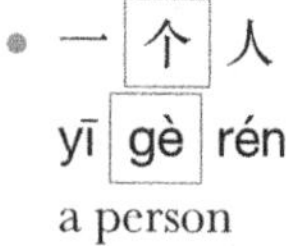

- 一 个 人
  yī gè rén
  a person
- 两 只 猫
  liǎng zhī māo
  two cats
- 三 条 鱼
  sān tiáo yú
  three fish

- 四 [杯] 牛奶
  sì [bēi] niúnǎi
  four glasses of milk
- 五 [瓶] 水
  wǔ [píng] shuǐ
  five bottles of water
- 六 [块] 巧克力
  liù [kuài] qiǎokèlì
  six pieces of chocolate
- 七 [盒] 茶叶
  qī [hé] cháyè
  seven boxes of tea leaves
- 八 [台] 电脑
  bā [tái] diànnǎo
  eight computers
- 九 [支] 玫瑰
  jiǔ [zhī] méiguī
  nine roses
- 十 [个] 美女
  shí [gè] měinǚ
  ten beautiful women

Also remember that there isn't a one-to-one relationship between nouns and measure words. One measure word can be used with several different nouns:

- 一 [条] 狗
  yī [tiáo] gǒu
  a dog
- 一 [条] 河
  yī [tiáo] hé
  a river
- 一 [条] 路
  yī [tiáo] lù
  a road

- 一 条 龙
  yī tiáo lóng
  a dragon
- 一 条 鱼
  yī tiáo yú
  a fish
- 一 条 短信
  yī tiáo duǎnxìn
  a text (message)

And one noun can take different measure words in different situations:

- 一 块 巧克力
  yī kuài qiǎokèlì
  a piece of chocolate
- 一 盒 巧克力
  yī hé qiǎokèlì
  a box of chocolate
- 一 颗 巧克力
  yī kē qiǎokèlì
  a small piece of chocolate

Similar to

- Age with "sui" (HSK1)
- Measure word "ge" (HSK1)
- Measure words in quantity questions (HSK1)
- Measure words for verbs (HSK2), page 116
- Measure words with "this" and "that" (HSK2), page 163
- Ordinal numbers with "di" (HSK2), page 165
- Approximating with sequential numbers (HSK3)

Measure words with "this" and "that"

In English, when you refer to "this table" or "that girl" you only need two words: "this" or "that" plus the noun you're referring to. In Chinese, though, you also need a measure word in the middle between the two. In the very beginning you can get away with using 个 (gè) for everything, but pretty soon you're going to have to start using other measure words in these simple phrases.

Structure

If you use 这 (zhè) or 那 (nà) before a noun, you also need to include a measure word before the noun.

 这 / 那 + Measure Word + Noun

Examples

Note: In this usage, the tone of 个 (gè) tends to soften, so it's represented below as a neutral tone.

- 那 个 人
  nà ge rén
  that person
- 这 本 书
  zhè běn shū
  this book
- 那 件 事
  nà jiàn shì
  that matter (in the sense of business, affair, or thing)
- 这 瓶 啤酒
  zhè píng píjiǔ
  this bottle of beer
- 那 个 房间
  nà ge fángjiān
  that room

那 台 电脑
nà tái diànnǎo
that new computer
这 只 猫
zhè zhī māo
that cat
那 条 河
nà tiáo hé
that river
这 件 衣服
zhè jiàn yīfu
this piece of clothing

Although we didn't get into it here, the same pattern holds true when you use 哪 (nǎ) to ask "which?"

Similar to

- Expressing "some" with "yixie" (HSK1)
- Measure word "ge" (HSK1)
- Measure words in quantity questions (HSK1)
- Measure words for counting (HSK2), page 160
- Measure words for verbs (HSK2), page 116

Ordinal numbers with "di"

Also known as: 序数 (xùshù), ordinals and sequence numbers.

We use ordinal numbers to express things like "number one" or "second," so mastering them in Chinese is important. Fortunately, they are also very easy to learn by just adding the prefix 第 (dì).

Basic Usage

In English, there are four different suffixes for ordinal numbers: *-st*, *-nd*, *-rd* and *-th*. Chinese makes things a lot simpler by using one prefix for all ordinal numbers: 第 (dì). This character is simply placed in front of the number:

Structure

Examples

Chinese	English
第一 dì-yī	The first
第二 dì-èr	The second
第三 dì-sān	The third
第四 dì-sì	The fourth
第五 dì-wǔ	The fifth
第六 dì-liù	The sixth
第七 dì-qī	The seventh
第八 dì-bā	The eighth

第九 dì-jiǔ	The ninth
第十 dì-shí	The tenth

Full Pattern with Measure Words

You can also add in a measure word and a noun to make the structure a bit fuller.

Structure

第 + Number + Measure Word + Noun

Examples

- 我是 第一 个 到公司的人。
  Wǒ shì dì-yī gè dào gōngsī de rén.
  I'm the first person that came to the office.
- 他要坐早上 第一 班 地铁去上班。
  Tā yào zuò zǎoshang dì-yī bān dìtiě qù shàngbān.
  He needs to take the first train in the morning to go to work.
- 小李是她的 第三 个 男朋友。
  Xiǎo Lǐ shì tā de dì-sān gè nánpéngyou.
  Little Li is her third boyfriend.
- 我的 第一 个 中文老师是美国人。
  Wǒ de dì-yī gè Zhōngwén lǎoshī shì Měiguó rén.
  My first Chinese teacher was American.
- 爸爸的 第一 个 手机是 NOKIA。
  Bàba de dì-yī gè shǒujī shì NOKIA.
  Dad's first cell phone was a Nokia.

- 你的 第一 个 工作是什么？
  Nǐ de dì-yī gè gōngzuò shì shénme?
  What was your first job?
- 到美国的 第二 个 月，我找到了工作。
  Dào Měiguó de dì-èr gè yuè, wǒ zhǎodào le gōngzuò .
  I found a job the second month I was in the USA.
- 第二 行 第五 个 汉字怎么读？
  Dì-èr háng dì-wǔ gè Hànzì zěnme dú?
  How do you read the fifth character from the second line?
- 这次考试，我是我们班 第一 。
  Zhè cì kǎoshì, wǒ shì wǒmen bān dì-yī.
  On this test, I was first in our class.
- 这次比赛，我们班 第一 ，他们班 第二 。
  Zhè cì bǐsài, wǒmen bān dì-yī, tāmen bān dì-èr.
  In this contest, our class is the first, their class is the second.

Note that there are some words that don't use measure words because they themselves are already measure words. For example: 天 (tiān), 年 (nián), 周 (zhōu), 次 (cì), etc.

- 第一 天 ，我们在宾馆里。
  Dì-yī tiān , wǒmen zài bīnguǎn lǐ.
  On the first day, we will be in the hotel.
- 来上海以后的 第二 年 ，他开了这家公司。
  Lái Shànghǎi yǐhòu de dì-èr nián , tā kāi le zhè jiā gōngsī.
  He started this company his second year after coming to Shanghai.
- 下个月的 第一 周 老板要出差。
  Xià gè yuè de dì-yī zhōu , lǎobǎn yào chūchāi.
  The boss needs to go on a business trip the first week of next month.
- 这是我 第一 次 去北京。
  Zhè shì wǒ dì-yī cì qù Běijīng.
  This is my first time going to Beijing.

Exceptions

Note that some nouns can form ordinals without 第 (dì). With these, the number can be used directly. For example, 七楼 (qī lóu) is "the seven*th* floor," even though there is no 第 (dì).

Chinese	English	Example
楼 lóu	floor (of a building)	七楼 qī lóu
层 céng	floor (of a building)	一层 yī céng

Similar to

- Age with "sui" (HSK1)
- Measure word "ge" (HSK1)
- Measure words for counting (HSK2), page 160

Affirmative-negative question

Also known as: 正反问句 (zhèng-fǎn wènjù) and alternative questions.

A common way to form questions in Chinese is to first use a verb in the positive, then repeat the same verb in its negative form, similar to how in English we can say, "Do you have money or not?" or "Have you or have you not been to the park?" This sentence pattern feels a lot more natural in Chinese than those admittedly awkward English equivalents, however.

Verb-Not-Verb

Structure

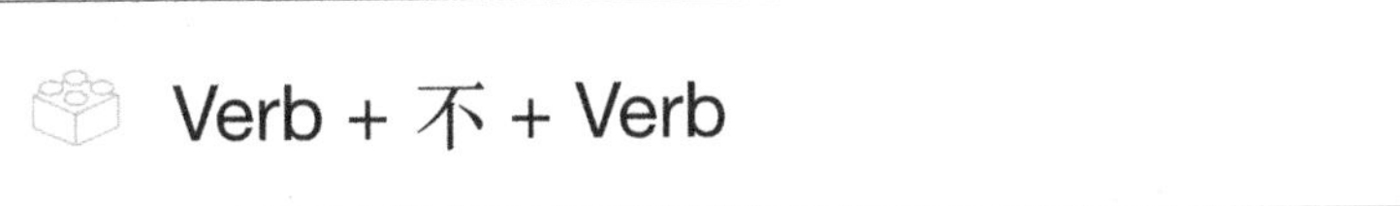

Examples

- 是不是？
  Shì bu shì?
  Is it (or not)?
- 他们 来不来？
  Tāmen lái bu lái?
  Are they going to come or not?
- 你 想不想 我？
  Nǐ xiǎng bu xiǎng wǒ?
  Do you or do you not miss me?
- 我们要去酒吧，你 去不去？
  Wǒmen yào qù jiǔbā, nǐ qù bu qù?
  We are going to the bar. Do you want to go?
- 我去买咖啡，你 要不要？
  Wǒ qù mǎi kāfēi, nǐ yào bu yào?
  I'm going to buy coffee. Do you want some?

Note that the question provides the listener with both possible answers: it's either "Verb" or "不 (bù) Verb."

Verb-Not-Verb with an Object

Structure

If you want to add an object after the verb, the general sentence structure is:

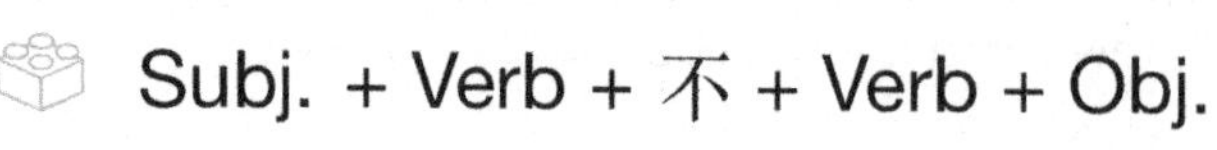

Subj. + Verb + 不 + Verb + Obj.

Examples

- 你 回不回 家？
  Nǐ huí bu huí jiā?
  Are you coming back home or not?
- 她 吃不吃 鱼？
  Tā chī bu chī yú?
  Does she eat fish?
- 你们 要不要 米饭？
  Nǐmen yào bu yào mǐfàn?
  Do you want rice?
- 你爸爸 喝不喝 酒？
  Nǐ bàba hē bu hē jiǔ?
  Does your dad drink alcohol or not?
- 今天老板 来不来 办公室？
  Jīntiān lǎobǎn lái bu lái bàngōngshì?
  Is the boss coming to the office today?

Adjective-Not-Adjective

Structure

It can also be done with adjectives (adjectives often behave like verbs in Chinese):

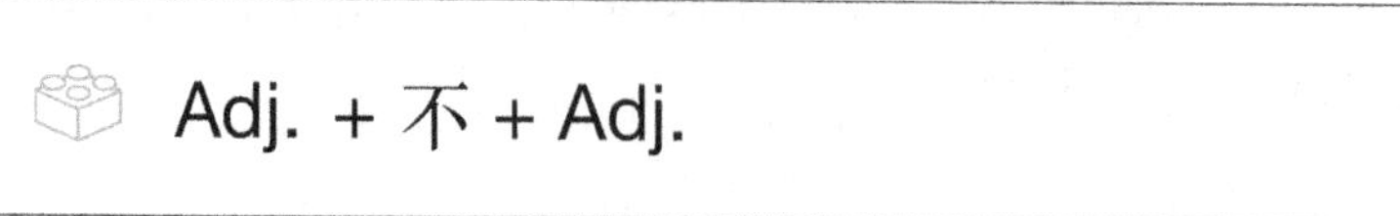

Adj. + 不 + Adj.

Examples

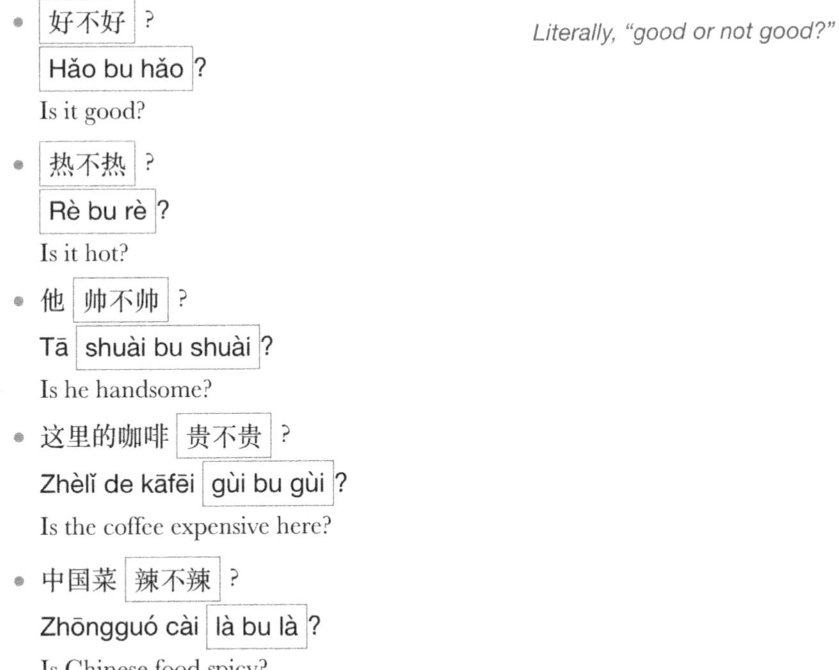

- 好不好？
  Hǎo bu hǎo?
  Is it good?

  Literally, "good or not good?"
- 热不热？
  Rè bu rè?
  Is it hot?
- 他帅不帅？
  Tā shuài bu shuài?
  Is he handsome?
- 这里的咖啡贵不贵？
  Zhèlǐ de kāfēi gùi bu gùi?
  Is the coffee expensive here?
- 中国菜辣不辣？
  Zhōngguó cài là bu là?
  Is Chinese food spicy?

Again, the question provides the listener with both possible answers: it's either "Adjective" or "不 (bù) Adjective."

These are something like adding tag questions in English, in this case "Are you an adult or not?" If you wanted to translate it very literally, it would be, "Are you or are you not an adult?" In any case, the structure is a very common way to ask questions in Chinese.

Two-Character Verbs and Adjectives

All of the verbs used so far have been single-character verbs. Using two-characters verbs in affirmative-negative questions is slightly trickier. You usually put 不 (bù) after just the first character, then put the entire verb. For example 喜不喜欢 (xǐ bu xǐhuan) is the usual question form of 喜欢 (xǐhuan). You can repeat the whole two-character verb twice, but it's more common (and more elegant) to insert 不 (bù) after the first character (and the same is generally true of two-character adjectives).

Structure

It can be done with verbs:

[First Character of Verb] + 不 + Verb

It can also be done with adjectives:

[First Character of Adj.] + 不 + Adj.

Examples

- 喜欢不喜欢？ *whole word repeated*
  Xǐhuan bu xǐhuan?
  Do you like it?
- 喜不喜欢？ *only the first character repeated*
  Xǐ bu xǐhuan?
  Do you like it?
- 高兴不高兴？ *whole word repeated*
  Gāoxìng bu gāoxìng?
  Are you happy?
- 高不高兴？ *only the first character repeated*
  Gāo bu gāoxìng?
  Are you happy?
- 他女朋友漂亮不漂亮？ *whole word repeated*
  Tā nǚpéngyou piàoliang bu piàoliang?
  Is his girlfriend pretty?
- 他女朋友漂不漂亮？ *only the first character repeated*
  Tā nǚpéngyou piào bu piàoliang?
  Is his girlfriend pretty?

- 中国菜 好吃不好吃？ *whole word repeated*
  Zhōngguó cài hǎochī bu hǎochī?
  Is Chinese food good?
- 中国菜 好不好吃？ *only the first character repeated*
  Zhōngguó cài hǎo bu hǎochī?
  Is Chinese food good?
- 那个地方 好玩不好玩？ *whole word repeated*
  Nàge dìfang hǎowán bu hǎowán?
  Is that place fun?
- 那个地方 好不好玩？ *only the first character repeated*
  Nàge dìfang hǎo bu hǎowán?
  Is that place fun?

有 (yǒu) is a Special Case

Structure

Because the verb 有 (yǒu) is negated with 没 (méi) and not 不 (bù), the structure for affirmative-negative questions with 有 (yǒu) is:

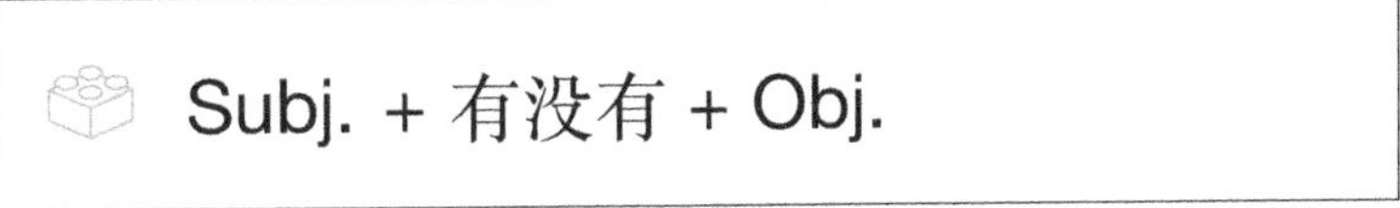

The possible answers are: "有 (yǒu)" or "没有 (méiyǒu)."

The questions could be be asking about current possession ("Do you have it or not?"), or to ask about verbs in the past ("Did you do it or not?").

Examples

- 你哥哥 有没有 女朋友？
  Nǐ gēge yǒu méiyǒu nǚpéngyou?
  Does your older brother have a girlfriend?
- 你们 有没有 孩子？
  Nǐmen yǒu méiyǒu háizi?
  Do you have children?

- 奶奶 有没有 坐过飞机?
  Năinai yǒu méiyǒu zuò guo fēijī?
  Has grandma been on a plane?
- 他 有没有 上过大学?
  Tā yǒu méiyǒu shàng guo dàxué?
  Has he been to college?

Similar to

- Comparing "bu" and "mei" (HSK1)
- Placement of question words (HSK1)
- Tag questions with "bu" (HSK2), page 181

Asking why with "zenme"

Aside from just meaning "how," 怎么 (zěnme) can also be used to ask "why" or "how come."

Basic Usage

With a Verb

Structure

Similar to the question word 为什么 (wèishénme), questions can also be asked with 怎么 (zěnme).

 Subj. + 怎么 + Verb + Obj. ?

This has similar connotations to saying "how come" in English. It not only asks why, but expresses some surprise at the situation, and in some cases even disagreement with it.

Examples

- 他 怎么 还没来?
  Tā zěnme hái méi lái?
  How come he's not here yet?
- 你们 怎么 打人?
  Nǐmen zěnme dǎ rén?
  How can you hit people?
- 他帮了你，你 怎么 不说"谢谢"?
  Tā bāng le nǐ, nǐ zěnme bù shuō "xièxie"?
  He helped you. How come you didn't say thank you?
- 你结婚的时候 怎么 不告诉我?
  Nǐ jiéhūn de shíhou zěnme bù gàosu wǒ?
  How come you didn't tell me when you got married?
- 我们还没开始吃，他 怎么 已经吃完了?
  Wǒmen hái méi kāishǐ chī, tā zěnme yǐjīng chī wán le?
  We haven't started eating yet. How come he has already finished eating?

- 今天是星期一，你 怎么 不去上班？
  Jīntiān shì Xīngqīyī, nǐ zěnme bù qù shàngbān?
  Today is Monday. Why aren't you going to work?

With an Adjective

Structure

In this case, it's most common to negate the adjective after 怎么 (zěnme).

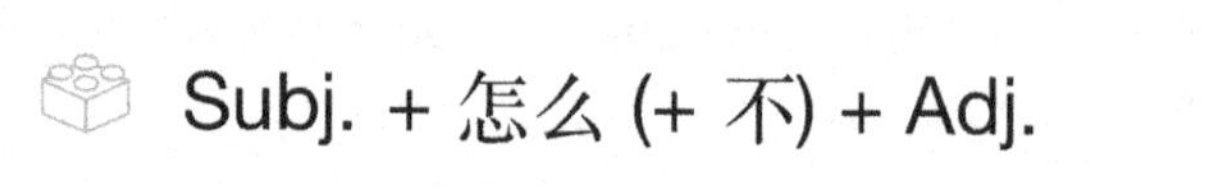

Subj. + 怎么 (+ 不) + Adj.

Examples

- 水 怎么 不热？
  Shuǐ zěnme bù rè?
  Why is the water not hot?
- 这里的川菜 怎么 不辣？
  Zhèlǐ de chuāncài zěnme bù là?
  Why is the Sichuan food here not spicy?
- 他亲了你，你 怎么 不高兴？
  Tā qīn le nǐ, nǐ zěnme bù gāoxìng?
  He kissed you. How come you're not happy?
- 她的小猫死了，她 怎么 不难过？
  Tā de xiǎomāo sǐ le, tā zěnme bù nánguò?
  Her kitten died. Why isn't she sad?
- 每天工作十二个小时，你 怎么 不累？
  Měi tiān gōngzuò shí'èr gè xiǎoshí, nǐ zěnme bù lèi?
  Every day you work 12 hours. Why are you not tired?

"Why So..." Usage

Structure

One pattern this use of 怎么 (zěnme) frequently appears in is with 这么 (zhème) or 那么 (nàme). (For more on 这么 (zhème) and 那么 (nàme), see adjectives with "name" and "zheme.")

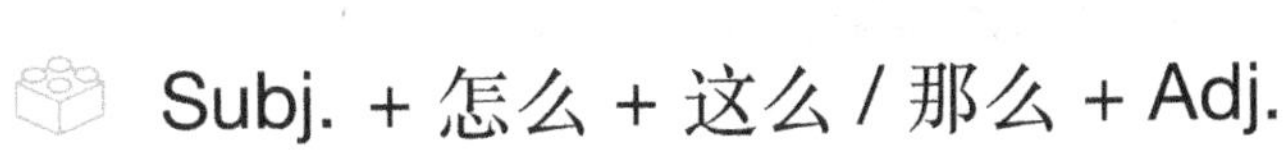

Subj. + 怎么 + 这么 / 那么 + Adj.

This use of 怎么 (zěnme) could be translated as either "how" or "why"; the actual meaning sort of falls in the fuzzy region between the two. In any case, it's used to express disbelief: *how can (something) be so (adjective)?!*

Examples

- 他 怎么 那么懒?
  Tā zěnme nàme lǎn?
  How can he be this lazy?
- 昨天 怎么 那么冷?
  Zuótiān zěnme nàme lěng?
  How could it be so cold yesterday?
- 这些人 怎么 这么吵?
  Zhèxiē rén zěnme zhème chǎo?
  How can these people so loud?
- 北京的空气 怎么 那么差?
  Běijīng de kōngqì zěnme nàme chà?
  How can the air in Beijing be so bad?
- 你的汉语 怎么 这么好?
  Nǐ de Hànyǔ zěnme zhème hǎo?
  How is your Mandarin so good?

Similar to

- Asking how something is with "zenmeyang" (HSK1)
- How to do something with "zenme" (HSK1)

Simple rhetorical questions

Rhetorical questions are ones where the speaker doesn't really expect an answer. The answer should be obvious, and the question is asked in order to make a point.

Structure

There are several very common types of rhetorical questions using basic words you already know:

This first one is the easiest and most common. It can be quite friendly, seemingly reminding the other person of a fact they seem to have (conveniently?) forgotten.

This one is often quite sarcastic, pointing out someone else's unrealistic expectations. (The obvious answer is "no" here.)

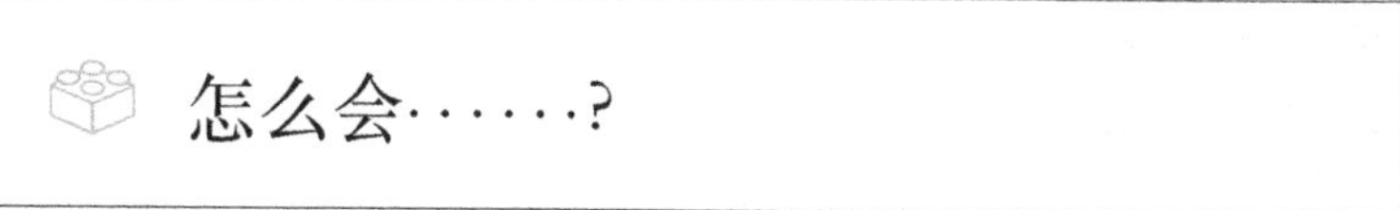

This second one has a tone of incredulity. The speaker clearly thinks this shouldn't have happened, or thought it couldn't have happened.

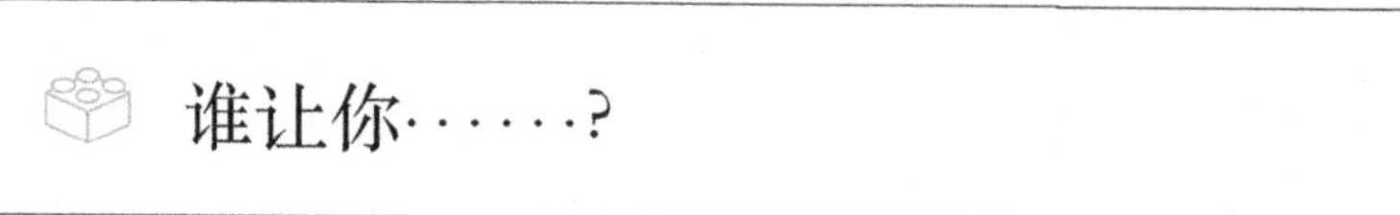

The third one is exclusively used by surly or annoyed people. It means "who told you to...?" or "who made you...?"

Examples

A: 你看到我的手机了吗?

Nǐ kàn dào wǒ de shǒujī le ma?

Have you seen my cell phone?

B: 不是 在桌子上 吗?

Bù shì zài zhuōzi shàng ma?

Isn't that it on the table?

A: 我们什么时候开会?

Wǒmen shénme shíhou kāi huì?

When are we having the meeting?

B: 不是 已经告诉你了 吗?

Bù shì yǐjīng gàosu nǐ le ma?

Haven't I told you that already?

A: 今天放假了，好开心。

Jīntiān fàngjià le, hǎo kāixīn.

We go on vacation today. I'm so happy!

B: 不是 明天放假 吗?

Bù shì míngtiān fàngjià ma?

Doesn't vacation start tomorrow?

A: 他又感冒了。

Tā yòu gǎnmào le.

He's caught another cold.

B: 他每天穿得都很少，能 不感冒 吗?

Tā měi tiān chuān de dōu hěn shǎo, néng bù gǎnmào ma?

He never dresses warmly. How could he not catch a cold?

A: 今天我可能会迟到。

Jīntiān wǒ kěnéng huì chídào.

I might be late today.

B: 你起得这么晚，能 不迟到 吗?

Nǐ qǐ de zhème wǎn, néng bù chídào ma?

You got up so late, how could you not be late?

A: 我点了很多菜，都是你爱吃的。

Wǒ diǎn le hěn duō cài, dōu shì nǐ ài chī de.

I ordered a bunch of food, all stuff that you like.

B: 晚上吃这么多菜，能 不胖 吗?

Wǎnshang chī zhème duō cài, néng bù pàng ma?

Eating so much food at night, how could I not gain weight?

A: 他们公司很厉害。

Tāmen gōngsī hěn lìhai.

Their company is really impressive.

B: 但是他们公司 怎么会 有这么笨的员工?

Dànshì tāmen gōngsī zěnme huì yǒu zhème bèn de yuángōng?

But then how can they have such a stupid employee?

A: 我收到了你的邮件。

Wǒ shōudào le nǐ de yóujiàn.

I received your text.

B: 那你 怎么会 不知道?

Nà nǐ zěnme huì bù zhīdao?

Then how is it that you don't know?

A: 我感觉最近有一点胖了。

Wǒ gǎnjué zuìjìn yǒu yīdiǎn pàng le.

I feel like I've gained some weight recently.

B: 谁让你 吃这么多?

Shéi ràng nǐ chī zhème duō?

Who made you eat so much?

Yes, this is totally mean in Chinese too, but people do say stuff like this.

A: 我找不到我的钥匙了。

Wǒ zhǎo bùdào wǒ de yàoshi le.

I can't find my key.

B: 谁让你 不放在包里。

Shéi ràng nǐ bù fàng zài bāo lǐ.

What stopped you from putting it in your bag?

Technically a question, but Chinese people often won't write the question mark on a sentence like this.

Tag questions with "bu"

In the same way you can tag questions with 吗 (ma)[1], tag questions can also be formed using 不 (bù). This is done by putting an affirmative-negative question[2] at the end of a sentence.

Structure

This can then be attached to the end of a sentence to form a tag question. Tag questions seek confirmation or acceptance of what has been said. In English, "right?" and "OK?" are often used as tag questions.

Examples

- 你会说中文，对不对？
  Nǐ huì shuō Zhōngwén, duì bu duì?
  You speak Chinese, right?
- 他是你的老板，对不对？
  Tā shì nǐ de lǎobǎn, duì bu duì?
  He's your boss, right?
- 我们是好朋友，对不对？
  Wǒmen shì hǎo péngyou, duì bu duì?
  We are good friends, right?
- 你昨天没回家，对不对？
  Nǐ zuótiān méi huíjiā, duì bu duì?
  You didn't come back home yesterday, right?
- 你有新女朋友了，是不是？
  Nǐ yǒu xīn nǚpéngyou le, shì bu shì?
  You have a new girlfriend, right?

1. Tag questions with "ma" (Grammar), page 183
2. Affirmative-negative question (Grammar), page 169

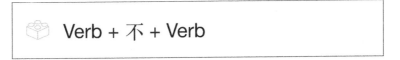

- 九点开会，是不是？
  Jiǔ diǎn kāihuì, shì bu shì?
  We are going to hold a meeting at 9, right?
- 你姓王，是不是？
  Nǐ xìng Wáng, shì bu shì?
  Your last name is Wang, is it not?
- 我们回家吧，好不好？
  Wǒmen huíjiā ba, hǎo bu hǎo?
  Let's go home, OK?
- 周末去看电影，好不好？
  Zhōumò qù kàn diànyǐng, hǎo bu hǎo?
  Let's go to a movie this weekend, OK?
- 你们明天来，好不好？
  Nǐmen míngtiān lái, hǎo bu hǎo?
  You come here tomorrow, OK?

Similar to

- Comparing "bu" and "mei" (HSK1)
- Affirmative-negative question (HSK2), page 169
- Tag questions with "ma" (HSK2), page 183

Tag questions with "ma"

As well as yes/no questions, you can also form tag questions with 吗 (ma). Tag questions are quick questions that are tagged on the end of a sentence to ask for confirmation. In English, this is often done with "right?" or negatively with "isn't it?"

The easiest way to do this in Chinese is to add some kind of confirmation word and 吗 (ma) on the end of the sentence.

Structure

As you can see below, the pattern typically involves words like 好 (hǎo), 对 (duì), 是 (shì), or 可以 (kěyǐ), followed by 吗 (ma).

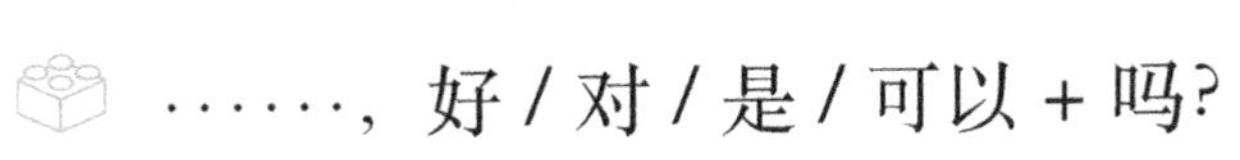

……，好 / 对 / 是 / 可以 + 吗？

By placing these on the end of a sentence, you can soften a suggestion or request confirmation.

Examples

- 这样做，对吗？
  Zhèyàng zuò, duì ma?
  Do it like this, right?
- 你们见过，对吗？
  Nǐmen jiàn guo, duì ma?
  You've met, right?
- 他们昨天都没去，是吗？
  Tāmen zuótiān dōu méi qù, shì ma?
  They didn't go yesterday, right?
- 你没来过，是吗？
  Nǐ méi lái guo, shì ma?
  You haven't been here, right?
- 你喜欢我妹妹，是吗？
  Nǐ xǐhuan wǒ mèimei, shì ma?
  You like my younger sister, huh?

- 我们去你家，好吗？
  Wǒmen qù nǐ jiā, hǎo ma?
  Let's go to your place, OK?
- 不要告诉他，好吗？
  Bùyào gàosu tā, hǎo ma?
  Don't tell him, OK?
- 今天我们都不喝酒，好吗？
  Jīntiān wǒmen dōu bù hējiǔ, hǎo ma?
  Let's all not drink alcohol today, OK?
- 我现在想去洗手间，可以吗？
  Wǒ xiànzài xiǎng qù xǐshǒujiān, kěyǐ ma?
  I want to go to the bathroom now. Is that OK?
- 妈妈，我要吃巧克力，可以吗？
  Māma, wǒ yào chī qiǎokèlì, kěyǐ ma?
  Mom, I want to eat chocolate. May I?

Similar to

- Questions with "ne" (HSK1, HSK3)
- Yes-no questions with "ma" (HSK1)
- Tag questions with "bu" (HSK2), page 181
- Advanced yes-no questions with "ma" (HSK4)

Cause and effect with "yinwei" and "suoyi"

You will often come across 因为…… 所以…… (yīnwèi... suǒyǐ...) in both written and spoken Chinese. This pattern will give your Chinese a clear logical structure, and can help make you more persuasive.

Using 因为 (yīnwèi) by Itself to Explain Causes

A common way to explain causes in Chinese is with 因为 (yīnwèi). This is equivalent to "because" in English. Usually 因为 (yīnwèi) will begin a new phrase in a sentence.

Structure

In this structure, we first state the result, and then give the reason in the next statement after the 因为 (yīnwèi).

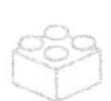 Result, 因为 + Reason

Examples

- 他学得很快，因为 他很聪明。
  Tā xué de hěn kuài, yīnwèi tā hěn cōngming.
  He learns fast because he is smart.
- 我爱吃四川菜，因为 很辣。
  Wǒ ài chī Sìchuān cài, yīnwèi hěn là.
  I love eating Sichuan food because it's very spicy.
- 我在学习中文，因为 我想去中国。
  Wǒ zài xuéxí Zhōngwén, yīnwèi wǒ xiǎng qù Zhōngguó.
  I am studying Chinese because I want to go to China.
- 我不喜欢她，因为 她不友好。
  Wǒ bù xǐhuan tā, yīnwèi tā bù yǒuhǎo.
  I don't like her because she is very unfriendly.
- 今天我们很忙，因为 有很多工作。
  Jīntiān wǒmen hěn máng, yīnwèi yǒu hěn duō gōngzuò.
  We are very busy today because we have lots of work.

Using 所以 (suǒyǐ) by Itself to Explain Results

Just as 因为 (yīnwèi) can be used to explain causes, 所以 (suǒyǐ) can be used to explain results. This is the equivalent of "so···" or "therefore···" in English.

Structure

This pattern is similar to the expression using both 因为 (yīnwèi) and 所以 (suǒyǐ), but it leaves out the beginning 因为 (yīnwèi). This structure is more informal.

 Reason, 所以 + Result

Examples

- 汉字太难了，所以 我不想学。

  Hànzì tài nán le, suǒyǐ wǒ bù xiǎng xué.

  Chinese characters are too hard, so I don't want to study them.

- 她很漂亮，所以 很多男孩喜欢她。

  Tā hěn piàoliang, suǒyǐ hěn duō nánhái xǐhuan tā.

  She is beautiful, so a lot of boys like her.

- 他找到工作了，所以 很高兴。

  Tā zhǎodào gōngzuò le, suǒyǐ hěn gāoxìng.

  He found a job so he's happy.

- 我太忙了，所以 没有时间给你打电话。

  Wǒ tài máng le, suǒyǐ méiyǒu shíjiān gěi nǐ dǎ diànhuà.

  I was too busy, so I didn't have time to give you a call.

- 我们公司有很多外国人，所以 我们要说英文。

  Wǒmen gōngsī yǒu hěn duō wàiguó rén, suǒyǐ wǒmen yào shuō Yīngwén.

  There are a lot of foreigners in our company, so we need to speak English.

Using 因为 (yīnwèi) and 所以 (suǒyǐ) Together

The full pattern 因为…… 所以…… (yīnwèi… suǒyǐ…) is used to clearly indicate cause and effect. They could be thought of as equating to: "Since happened, so happened." It sounds weird to use both "since" and "so" in one sentence in English, but it makes everything crystal clear in Chinese.

Structure

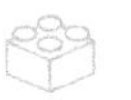

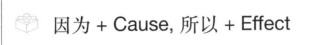

因为 + Cause, 所以 + Effect

This expresses that because of *cause*, therefore there is a *result*.

Examples

- 因为 我有一个中国女朋友，所以 我要学中文。
  Yīnwèi wǒ yǒu yī gè Zhōngguó nǚpéngyou, suǒyǐ wǒ yào xué Zhōngwén.
  Since I have a Chinese girlfriend, I need to study Chinese.
- 因为 他生病了，所以 没去上课。
  Yīnwèi tā shēngbìng le, suǒyǐ méi qù shàngkè.
  Since he was sick, he didn't go to class.
- 因为 我很累，所以 要休息。
  Yīnwèi wǒ hěn lèi, suǒyǐ yào xiūxi.
  I'm very tired, so I want to rest.
- 因为 太远了，所以 我不想去。
  Yīnwèi tài yuǎn le, suǒyǐ wǒ bù xiǎng qù.
  Since it's too far, I don't want to go.
- 因为 太忙，所以 我们没有时间吃中饭。
  Yīnwèi tài máng, suǒyǐ wǒmen méiyǒu shíjiān chī zhōngfàn.
  We were too busy, so none of us had time to eat lunch.

Similar to

- Expressing "then…" with "name" (HSK3)
- Expressing "as a result" with "jieguo" (HSK4)
- Expressing "since" with "jiran" (HSK4)
- Expressing "therefore" with "yinci" (HSK4)
- Stating the effect before the cause (HSK5)
- Using "because" with "er" to indicate effect (HSK5)
- Express an action and its effect by using "tongguo… shi" (HSK6)

Expressing "about to happen" with "le"

Remember that 了 (le) is not only for the past! When something is *about to happen,* you can also indicate this using 了 (le). Normally it is paired with a 快 (kuài), 快要 (kuàiyào) or a 要 (yào). This is a special form of using 了 to indicate a change of situation.

快⋯⋯了 (kuài... le) with Verbs

When using 快⋯⋯了 (kuài... le) with verbs, it takes on a meaning similar to the English "just about to." Normally you can add 要 (yào) before the verb.

Structure

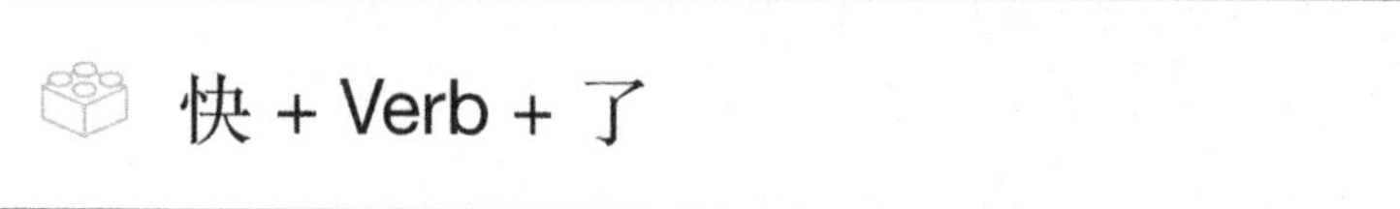

快要 + Verb + 了

Examples

- 我们 快 到 了 。
  Wǒmen kuài dào le.
  We're almost there.
- 快 下雨 了 。
  Kuài xiàyǔ le.
  It's going to rain soon.
- 快要 过年 了 ，你什么时候回家?
  Kuài yào guònián le, nǐ shénme shíhou huíjiā?
  It's almost Chinese New Year. When are you going back to your hometown?
- 我女朋友 快要 过生日 了 。
  Wǒ nǚpéngyou kuài yào guò shēngrì le.
  My girlfriend is about to have her birthday.

- 快 下车 了 ，你再等一会儿。
  Kuài xiàchē le, nǐ zài děng yīhuìr.
  We're about to get off. Just wait a little while.

Notice that for some translations, it's more natural to use the English word "almost" instead of "soon."

快⋯⋯了 (kuài... le) with Adjectives

In this structure, 快⋯⋯了 (kuài... le) is closer to the meaning of "almost" in English.

Structure

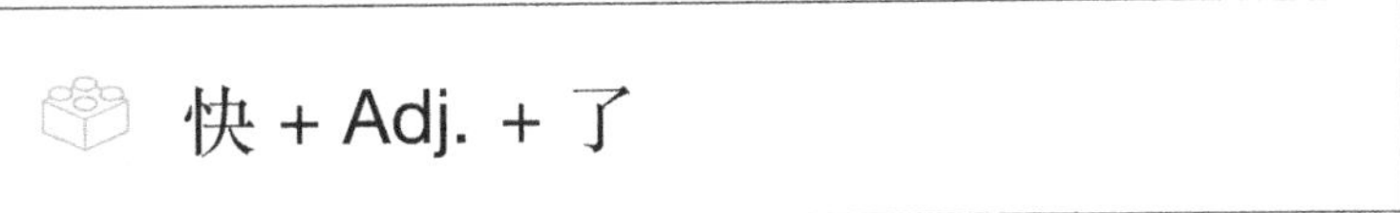

快 + Adj. + 了

Examples

- 天 快 黑 了 。
  Tiān kuài hēi le.
  It's almost getting dark.
- 我 快 好 了 。
  Wǒ kuài hǎo le.
  I'm almost ready.
- 饭 快 凉 了 。
  Fàn kuài liáng le.
  The food is about to be cold.
- 这些脏衣服 快 臭 了 。
  Zhèxiē zāng yīfu kuài chòu le.
  These dirty clothes are about to smell bad.
- 不能再喝了，我 快 醉 了 。
  Bù néng zài hē le, wǒ kuài zuì le.
  I can't drink another, I am almost drunk.

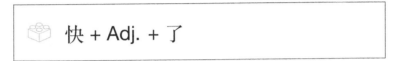

要……了 (yào... le) with Verbs

Structure

You can also just use 要 (yào) before the verb, without 快 (kuài).

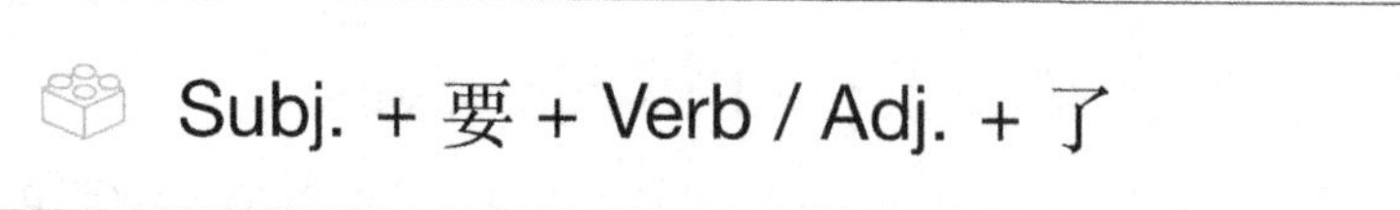

Note that occasionally you'll see adjectives (instead of verbs) in this pattern as well.

Examples

- 我 要 生气 了 ！
  Wǒ yào shēngqì le!
  I'm going to get angry!
- 他们的孩子 要 出生 了 。
  Tāmen de háizi yào chūshēng le.
  Their child is about to be born.
- 9 点了，超市 要 关门 了 。
  Jiǔ diǎn le, chāoshì yào guānmén le.
  It's 9 o'clock. The supermarket is about to close.
- 我最好的朋友 要 结婚 了 ！
  Wǒ zuìhǎo de péngyou yào jiéhūn le!
  My best friend is about to get married!
- 圣诞节 要 到 了 ，你有什么打算？
  Shèngdànjié yào dào le, nǐ yǒu shénme dǎsuàn?
  It's almost Christmas. What plans do you have?

Similar to

- Auxiliary verb "yao" and its multiple meanings (HSK2), page 102
- Expressing "about to" with "jiuyao" (HSK2), page 14
- Expressing "be going to" with "yao" (HSK2), page 106

Expressing "everything" with "shenme dou"

什么…… 都 (shénme... dōu) is a pattern often used to express "all" or "everything." Because it's not just one word, though, it can be a little tricky to get the hang of at first.

Basic Usage

Structure

In this structure, 都 (dōu) is more frequently used than 也 (yě)。

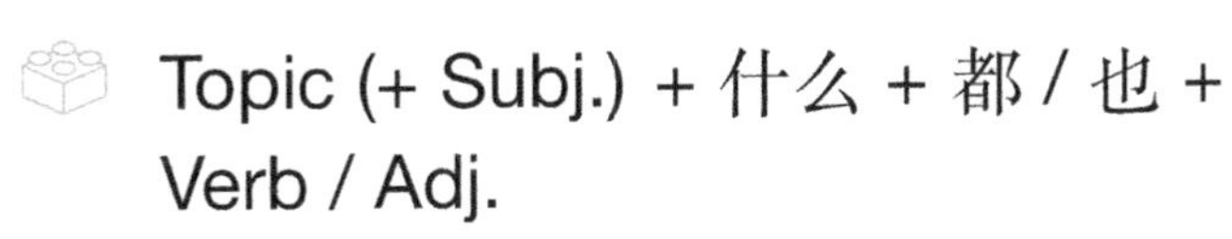

Topic (+ Subj.) + 什么 + 都 / 也 + Verb / Adj.

In some sentences, there will be a subject after the topic in the pattern above. See the following sentences for examples.

Examples

When used in the positive sense, it is more natural to follow 什么 (shénme) with 都 (dōu) rather than 也 (yě) to express "everything."

- 我觉得这里的菜 什么 都 好吃。
  Wǒ juéde zhèlǐ de cài shénme dōu hǎochī.
  I think everything is delicious here.
- 中国的历史爸爸 什么 都 知道。
  Zhōngguó de lìshǐ bàba shénme dōu zhīdào.
  My dad knows everything about Chinese history.
- 工作的事情老公 什么 都 跟我说。
  Gōngzuò de shìqing lǎogōng shénme dōu gēn wǒ shuō.
  My husband tells me everything about work stuff.
- 妈妈做的菜我 什么 都 喜欢。
  Māma zuò de cài wǒ shénme dōu xǐhuan.
  I like everything that mom cooks.
- 我女朋友觉得外国的东西 什么 都 好。
  Wǒ nǚpéngyou juéde wàiguó de dōngxi shénme dōu hǎo.
  My girlfriend thinks that all foreign things are good.

Structure with a Noun

Structure

什么 + Noun + 都 + Verb

Examples

- 我们什么果汁都喝。
  Wǒmen shénme guǒzhī dōu hē.
  We drink any kind of fruit juice.
- 她什么衣服都是黑色的。
  Tā shénme yīfu dōu shì hēisè de.
  All of her clothes are black.
- 妈妈做的什么菜都好吃。
  Māma zuò de shénme cài dōu hǎochī.
  All of the dishes mom makes are tasty.
- 我男朋友什么运动都喜欢。
  Wǒ nánpéngyou shénme yùndòng dōu xǐhuan.
  My boyfriend likes all kinds of sports.
- 你不应该什么话都跟他说。
  Nǐ bù yīnggāi shénme huà dōu gēn tā shuō.
  You shouldn't tell him everything.

Negative Structure

Structures

The negative structure simply adds a 不 (bù) or a 没 (méi) after the 都 (dōu) / 也 (yě). Instead of "all" or "everything," this expresses "none" or "not any."

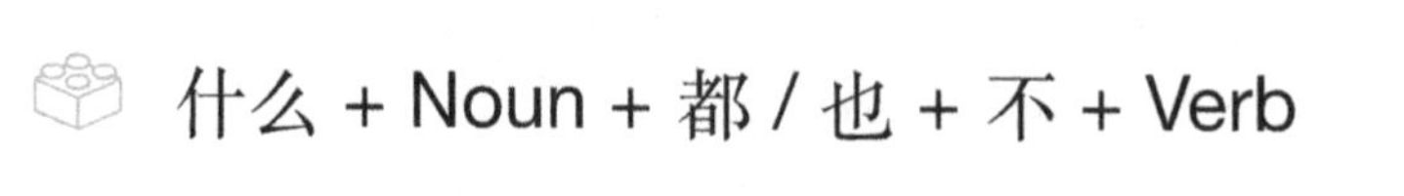

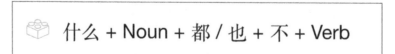

什么 + Noun + 都 / 也 + 不 + Verb

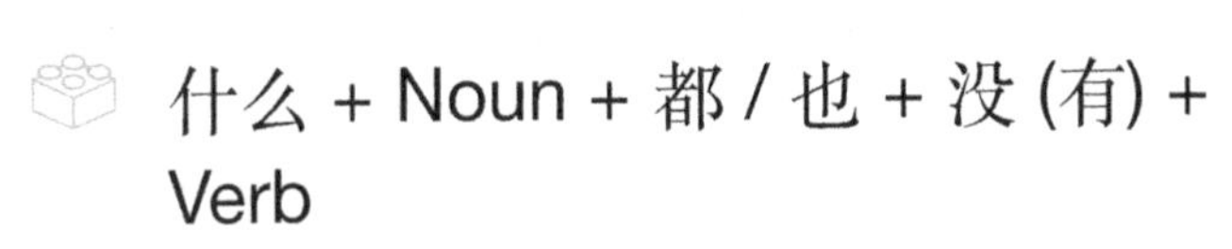

Examples

- 生病以后，爸爸什么酒都不能喝了。
  Shēngbìng yǐhòu, bàba shénme jiǔ dōu bù néng hē le.
  After dad got sick, he can't drink any kind of alcohol.
- 老板现在很生气，什么人也不见。
  Lǎobǎn xiànzài hěn shēngqì, shénme rén yě bù jiàn.
  The boss is very angry. He's doesn't want to see anybody.
- 今天我不舒服，什么东西都没吃。
  Jīntiān wǒ bù shūfu, shénme dōngxi dōu méi chī.
  Today I don't feel well, so I didn't eat anything.
- 昨天开会的时候，她什么话也没说。
  Zuótiān kāihuì de shíhou, tā shénme huà yě méi shuō.
  She didn't say anything at yesterday's meeting.
- 你在家里怎么什么事都不做？
  Nǐ zài jiālǐ zěnme shénme shì dōu bù zuò?
  How come you haven't done anything at home?

Similar to

- Expressing "every" with question words (HSK3, HSK4)
- Expressing "not at all" with "yidianr ye bu" (HSK4)

Expressing "stop doing" with "bie... le"

You may know how to make negative commands with "bie,"[1] but what if someone is already doing it? The pattern 别……了 (bié... le) is all you need to tell someone to *STOP DOING THAT* (which they're already doing).

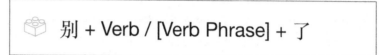

Structure

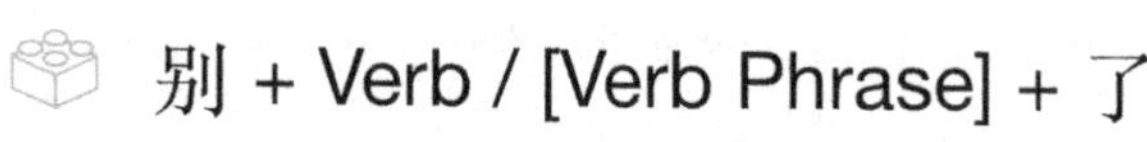

Instead of just a verb, it can also be a verb phrase.

Examples

- 别说了，我不想听。
  Bié shuō le, wǒ bù xiǎng tīng.
  Stop talking. I don't want to listen.
- 别问了，我不想说。
  Bié wèn le, wǒ bù xiǎng shuō.
  Stop asking. I don't want to say.
- 别做了，明天做吧。
  Bié zuò le, míngtiān zuò ba.
  Stop doing it. Do it tomorrow.
- 别看了，睡觉！
  Bié kàn le, shuìjiào!
  Stop watching. Go to sleep!
- 别哭了！
  Bié kū le!
  Stop crying!
- 别笑了，别人都在看你。
  Bié xiào le, biérén dōu zài kàn nǐ.
  Stop laughing. Other people are looking at you.

---

1. Negative commands with "bie" (Grammar), page 34

- 别 吃 了，我们要迟到了。
  Bié chī le, wǒmen yào chídào le.
  Stop eating. We're going to be late.
- 别 玩 了，去写作业。
  Bié wán le, qù xiě zuòyè.
  Stop playing. Do your homework.
- 别 喝 了，你已经醉了。
  Bié hē le, nǐ yǐjīng zuì le.
  Stop drinking. You're already drunk.

Other Meaning

The "别 verb 了" pattern can also be used to negate the other person's suggestion or try to change their idea. The difference between this usage and the previous example is that the action has not happened yet. A few examples:

- 别 买 了，太贵了！
  Bié mǎi le, tài guì le!
  Don't buy it. It's too expensive!

  In this case, the person probably isn't actually paying, but she or he is thinking about it.
- 别 做饭 了，出去吃吧。
  Bié zuòfàn le, chūqù chī ba.
  Let's go out for dinner instead of cook.

  In this case, the person probably isn't actually cooking, but she or he is thinking about it.
- 下雨了，别 出去 了。
  Xiàyǔ le, bié chūqù le.
  It's raining. Let's stay inside instead of going out.

  In this case, the person hasn't left yet, but she or he is thinking about going out.

The "shi... de" construction for indicating purpose

There are many ways to explain why you are doing something or what an object is used for. One of the more natural ways just happens to involve 是……的. This is a different usage from the "classic" 是……的 pattern.

A Person as Subject

Structure

If the subject is a person, there is often a 来 or 去 after the 是, indicating direction like "coming here" or "going there."

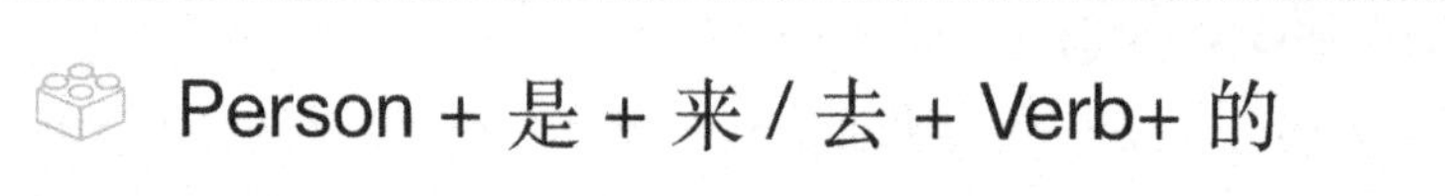

Person + 是 + 来 / 去 + Verb+ 的

Examples

- 我是来玩的。
  Wǒ shì lái wán de.
  I came for fun.
- 我们都是去出差的。
  Wǒmen dōu shì qù chūchāi de.
  We are all going on business trips.
- 他们都是来实习的。
  Tāmen dōu shì lái shíxí de.
  They all came here to do internships.
- 你真的是来帮我们的吗?
  Nǐ zhēnde shì lái bāng wǒmen de ma?
  Are you really here to help us?
- 我们不是去玩的，是去做调查的。
  Wǒmen bù shì qù wán de, shì qù zuò diàochá de.
  We're not going for fun. We're going to do research.

A Thing as Subject

Structure

If the subject is a thing, 用来 is often used. Look at the examples below for some more clarification.

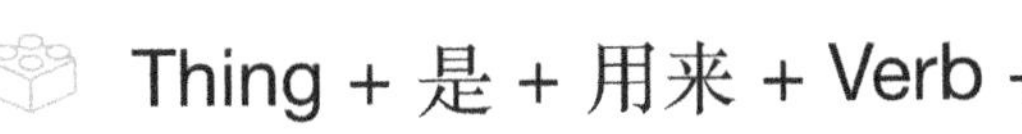
Thing + 是 + 用来 + Verb + 的

or

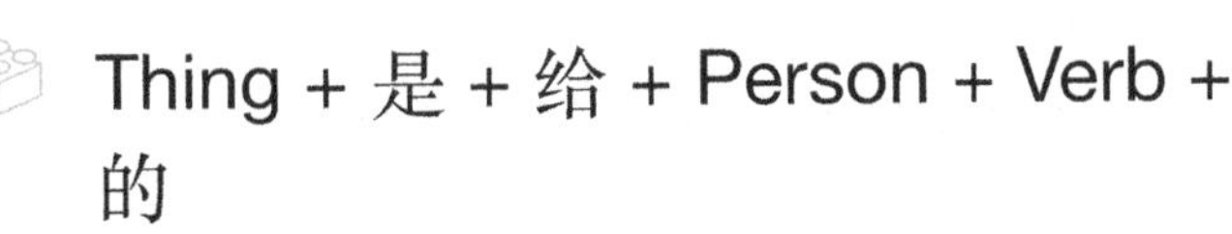
Thing + 是 + 给 + Person + Verb + 的

Examples

- 这种菜是用来做汤的。
  Zhè zhǒng cài shì yònglái zuò tāng de.
  This kind of vegetable is for making soup.
- 这个房间是给客人住的。
  Zhège fángjiān shì gěi kèrén zhù de.
  This room is for our guest to stay in.
- 这些钱是给孩子上大学的。
  Zhèxiē qián shì gěi háizi shàng dàxué de.
  This money is for our child's college education.
- 这些礼物是给客户准备的。
  Zhèxiē lǐwù shì gěi kèhù zhǔnbèi de.
  These presents have been prepared for the clients.
- 钱是用来花的，不是用来省的。
  Qián shì yònglái huā de, bù shì yònglái shěng de.
  Money is for spending, not for saving.

Similar to

- The “shi... de” construction for emphasizing details (HSK1)
- The “shi... de” patterns: an overview (HSK2), page 198

The "shi... de" patterns: an overview

An intermediate student of Chinese should be aware of the classic "shi... de" construction. It's important to learn and use. But don't be tempted to think that the "official" 是……的 (shì... de) pattern is the only way that 是 and 的 can work together in a sentence! There are multiple ways to use 是 and 的 together, and they can be used for different purposes. This article helps break down the various uses of 是……的 and tackle the confusion head-on.

Omitting a Noun with 的

This is the most simple way to use 是 with 的: you drop the noun and let 的 represent it. This usage requires context; otherwise the other person won't know what noun you are referring to. Having the 的 take the place of the noun is sort of like the way we say "one" or "it" in English. It's a basic substitution, but it's one that is very common and very helpful in everyday Chinese.

A: 你也是大学生？你 是 什么专业 的 ？
Nǐ yě shì dàxuéshēng? Nǐ shì shénme zhuānyè de?
Are you also a college student? What's your major?

B: 我 是 中文专业 的 。
Wǒ shì Zhōngwén zhuānyè de.
My major is Chinese.

Used with Distinguishing Words

If you're a good student, you learned the classic pattern for simple sentences using adjectives long ago (you know, the 你很漂亮 type), and you know that you're ***not*** supposed to use 是 in these sentences. But then you may have later come across some sentence patterns–apparently using adjectives–where you ***have*** to use 是 (and also 的). These are sentences that use a special type of word (you might think of it as a special class of adjectives, if that helps) called distinguishing words.

Structure

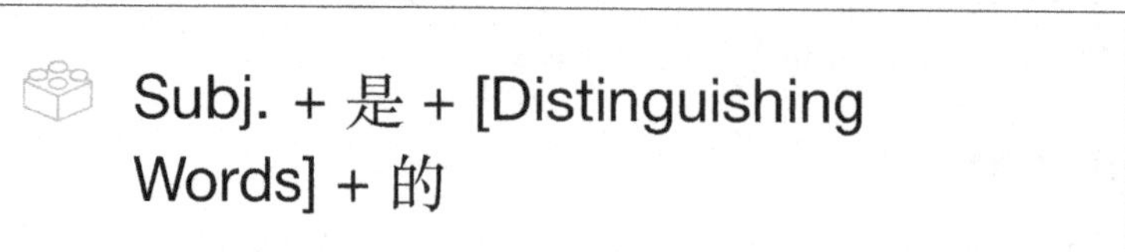

Examples

Pay attention to the "distinguishing words" between 是 and 的.

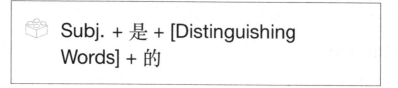

- 这个苹果 是 坏 的 。
  Zhège píngguǒ shì huài de.
  This apple is bad.
- 你错了，那个人 是 女 的 。
  Nǐ cuò le, nàge rén shì nǚ de.
  You are mistaken. That person is a woman.
- 他家的家具都 是 中式 的 。
  Tā jiā de jiājù dōu shì Zhōng shì de.
  The furniture in his house is all in Chinese style.

Other "distinguishing words" include colors, materials, sexes, and other categories that can have no degree.

The Classic Construction

Structure

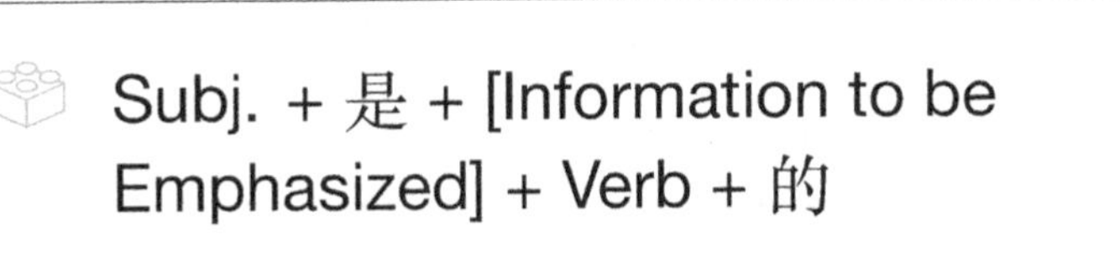

Subj. + 是 + [Information to be Emphasized] + Verb + 的

This classic pattern is the one for emphasizing certain *details* about events in the *past*. It's often used to ask pointed questions about past events, and then to answer those questions. Usually, the situation is already established, and the speakers are trying to get more specific clarification, such as when, where, or how the action took place. When this is the case, the phrase that follows the 是 is the part of the situation that is being emphasized.

It is also important to know that you can't use 了 in this type of sentence. 了 only tells you that the action is completed, not any of the other details that this construction is looking for. Since it is already understood that the action took place, the 了 is unhelpful and inappropriate. A more complete explanation of this particular usage can be found in the article on 是……的 for emphasizing details.

Examples

The examples below share the theme: 我在上海学了两年中文. Each sentence has a different aspect of the situation being emphasized.

A: 你 是 什么时候 开始学中文 的 ？
Nǐ shì shénme shíhou kāishǐ xué Zhōngwén de?
A: When was it that you started studying Chinese?

B: 我 是 两年前 开始学中文 的 。
Wǒ shì liǎng nián qián kāishǐ xué Zhōngwén de.
It was two years ago that I started studying Chinese.

A: 你 是 在哪里 学 的 中文?
Nǐ shì zài nǎlǐ xué de Zhōngwén?
Where is it that you study Chinese?

B: 我 是 在上海 学 的 中文。
Wǒ shì zài Shànghǎi xué de Zhōngwén.
It's in Shanghai that I study Chinese.

In the example above, you might have noticed something funny with the object of the verb. In this construction, if the verb is transitive (it takes an object), then the object can be placed either before or after the 的 without affecting the meaning. Take a look at the example below:

A: 昨天你 是 怎么 回 的 家?
Zuótiān nǐ shì zěnme huí de jiā?
How did you come back yesterday?

B: 昨天我 是 打车 回家 的 。
Zuótiān wǒ shì dǎchē huíjiā de.
I went home by taxi yesterday.

It's correct to put the 的 before *or* after the 家 in both of those sentences.

Used for Indicating Purpose or Intent

Structure

When explaining "what you came for" or "what you want to do," it's common to use yet another type of 是⋯⋯的 construction.

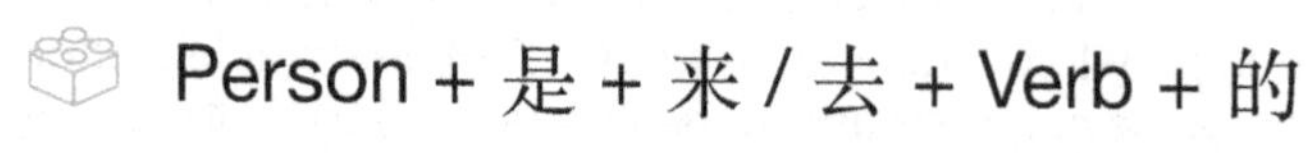
Person + 是 + 来 / 去 + Verb + 的

When expressing a purpose, 是 and 的 are often used together with 用来, especially when the subject is a thing.

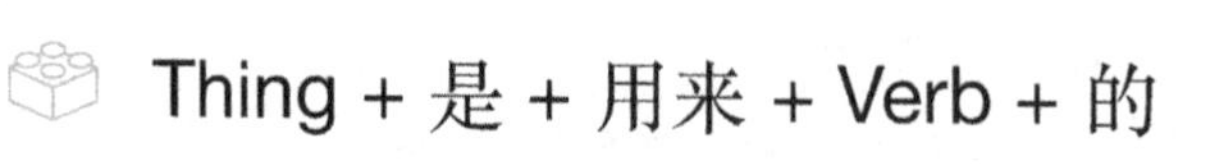
Thing + 是 + 用来 + Verb + 的

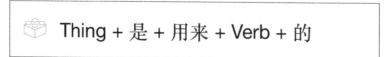

Examples

- 我是来实习的。
  Wǒ shì lái shíxí de.
  I came here to do an internship.
- 钱是用来花的，不是用来省的。
  Qián shì yònglái huā de, bù shì yònglái shěng de.
  Money is for spending, not for saving.

Used for Talking about What People Do

This pattern can also be used to talk about what kind of work people do:

A: 我是教汉语的。你是做什么的？
Wǒ shì jiāo Hànyǔ de. Nǐ shì zuò shénme de?
I teach Chinese. What kind of work do you do?

B: 我是送外卖的。
Wǒ shì sòng wàimài de.
I'm a take-out delivery guy.

Used for a Tone of Strong Affirmation

Sometimes you can use 的 to really add a kick to your responses, making them stronger. You might even hear Chinese people reply with just 是的 which means "That's right." This usage is similar to the way that English speakers might stress the word "is" in sentences like "It *is* my food." When used to express affirmation, 会, 能, and 可以 are often used as well. Again, the 是 is optional.

- 这个东西是可以吃的。
  Zhège dōngxi shì kěyǐ chī de.
  This thing is edible.
- 我会去的。
  Wǒ huì qù de.
  I will go.
- 我们能做到的。
  Wǒmen néng zuòdào de.
  We can do it.

Similar to

- The "shi… de" construction for emphasizing details (HSK1)
- The "shi… de" construction for indicating purpose (HSK2), page 196
- Using "de" (modal particle) (HSK4)

Expressing "every time" with "mei" and "dou"

每次……都……(měi cì... dōu...) is a pattern used to express "every time." Translating from English, you might feel that the only part really needed is 每次 (měi cì), since it literally means "every time." This is incorrect! Not only is the adverb 都 (dōu) *required*, but it's arguably more vital than the 每次 (měi cì)! So it's important to get used to using both parts.

Structure

This pattern actually builds on the basic 每……都……pattern[1], which you should already know. In this grammar structure, we go beyond just saying things like "every person" or "every day," and focus on what happens ***every time** a certain action is done.*

 每次 + Event 1 + 都 + Event 2

Examples

- 她 每次 来我家 都 带花。
  Tā měi cì lái wǒ jiā dōu dài huā.
  She brings flowers every time she visits me.
- 为什么 每次 我来他 都 不在?
  Wèishénme měi cì wǒ lái tā dōu bù zài?
  How come he's not here every time I come?
- 我 每次 玩这个游戏 都 输。
  Wǒ měi cì wán zhège yóuxì dōu shū.
  Every time I play this game, I lose.
- 你怎么 每次 吃火锅 都 拉肚子?
  Nǐ zěnme měicì chī huǒguō dōu lādùzi?
  How come you have diarrhea every time you eat hotpot?
- 他 每次 迟到 都 说因为堵车。
  Tā měicì chídào dōu shuō yīnwèi dǔchē.
  Every time he's late, he says it's because of bad traffic.

---

1. Expressing "every" with "mei" (Grammar), page 158

- 我 每次 经过这家店 都 会进去看看。
  Wǒ měi cì jīngguò zhè jiā diàn dōu huì jìnqù kànkan.
  Every time I pass this shop, I go inside and take a look.
- 我妹妹 每次 打针 都 哭。
  Wǒ mèimei měicì dǎzhēn dōu kū.
  My little sister cries every time she has to get a shot.
- 每次 遇到生词他 都 要查字典。
  Měi cì yùdào shēngcí tā dōu yào chá zìdiǎn.
  Every time he comes across a new word, he looks it up in the dictionary.
- 每次 编辑 都 要保存。
  Měi cì biānjí dōu yào bǎocún.
  Every time you edit, you need to save it.
- 爸爸 每次 出差 都 给我买礼物。
  Bàba měi cì chūchāi dōu gěi wǒ mǎi lǐwù.
  Dad buys presents for me every time he goes on business trips.

Similar to

- The "all" adverb "dou" (HSK1)
- Emphasizing quantity with "dou" (HSK2), page 11
- Expressing "every" with "mei" (HSK2), page 158
- Measure words for verbs (HSK2), page 116

Expressing "much more" in comparisons

If you want to up the contrast of your comparisons, you might want to express "much more." You can do this using 多 (duō), but did you know there are actually three different ways to do it?

Structure

As well as expressing that two things differ, you might want to go further and say that they differ **a lot** by adding 很多 (hěn duō), 多了 (duō le), or 得多 (de duō). This is like saying that one thing is *much more Adj.* than another in English.

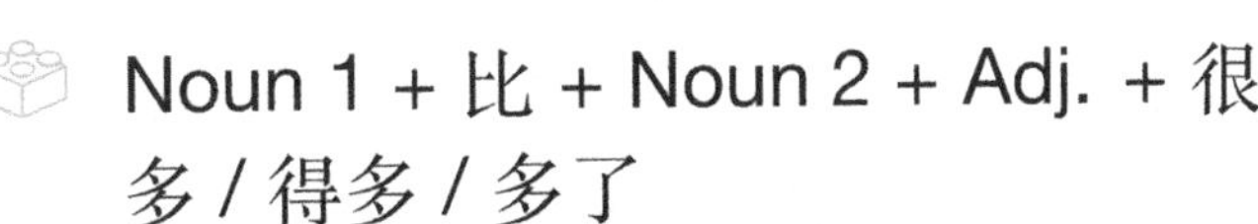

Noun 1 + 比 + Noun 2 + Adj. + 很多 / 得多 / 多了

Examples

- 拼音 比 汉字容易 很多 。

  Pīnyīn bǐ Hànzì róngyì hěn duō .

  Pinyin is much easier than Chinese characters.

- 坐高铁 比 坐飞机方便 很多 。

  Zuò gāotiě bǐ zuò fēijī fāngbiàn hěn duō .

  It's much more convenient to take the high-speed train than the airplane.

- 这个女老师 比 那个男老师严格 得多 。

  Zhège nǚ lǎoshī bǐ nàge nán lǎoshī yángé de duō .

  This female teacher is much stricter than that male teacher.

- 我老婆的工资 比 我高 得多 。

  Wǒ lǎopo de gōngzī bǐ wǒ gāo de duō .

  My wife's salary is much higher than mine.

- 你 比 我有经验 多了 。

  Nǐ bǐ wǒ yǒu jīngyàn duō le .

  You're much more experienced than me.

- 你们 比 我们幸运 多了 。
  Nǐmen bǐ wǒmen xìngyùn duō le .
  You're much luckier than us.
- 他打篮球 比 我厉害 多了 。
  Tā dǎ lánqiú bǐ wǒ lìhai duō le .
  He plays basketball much better than I do.

Short Form with 多了

Given sufficient context, it's possible to use 多了 without the full comparison pattern. 多了 is the only one of the three "much more" phrases introduced in this article which can be used this way.

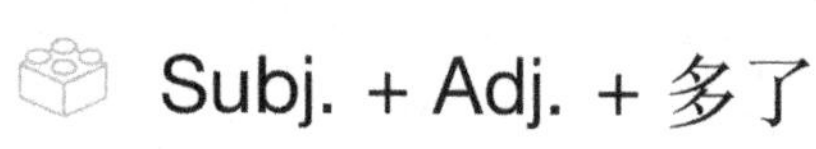

Subj. + Adj. + 多了

A few examples:

- 我的感冒好 多了 。
  Wǒ de gǎnmào hǎo duō le .
  My cold is getting much better.
  We both know I've had this bad cold.
- 最近天气暖和 多了 。
  Zuìjìn tiānqì nuǎnhuo duō le .
  It's been much warmer lately.
  We're both aware of recent weather, obviously.
- 上大学以后，她成熟 多了 。
  Shàng dàxué yǐhòu, tā chéngshú duō le .
  She became much more mature after she went to college.
  We both know how immature she used to be.

Similar to

- Basic comparisons with "bi" (HSK2), page 86
- Expressing "a little too" with "you dian" (HSK2), page 38
- Expressing "compared with" using "gen" (HSK3)
- Expressing "rather" with "bijiao" (HSK3)
- Basic comparisons with "bu bi" (HSK5)
- Expressing "a bit too" (HSK5)

Expressing "although" with "suiran" and "danshi"

The grammar pattern 虽然…… 但是…… (suīrán... dànshì...) is one of the most commonly used patterns in Chinese, especially in written Chinese. You can think of it as meaning "although," but unlike in English, you still need to follow it up with a "but" word in Chinese.

Structure

虽然…… 但是…… expresses that while the former part of the sentence is true, there is an adverse reaction in the latter part.

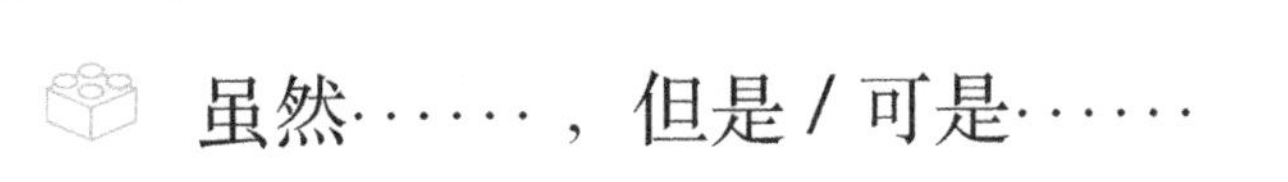

Simply put, the pattern means, *although..., but...* In English, you wouldn't normally need the "but" there, but it is required in Chinese. Be aware that 可是 can be used interchangeably with 但是 for the "but" part. Also note that 还是 can be used after 但是 for emphasis, meaning "still."

Examples

- 虽然外面很冷，可是里面很暖和。
  Suīrán wàimiàn hěn lěng, kěshì lǐmiàn hěn nuǎnhuo.
  Although it's cold outside, it's warm inside.
- 这件衣服虽然有点贵，但是质量很好。
  Zhè jiàn yīfu suīrán yǒudiǎn guì, dànshì zhìliàng hěn hǎo.
  Although this piece of clothing is a little expensive, the quality is good.
- 他虽然不想去，但是还是去了。
  Tā suīrán bù xiǎng qù, dànshì háishì qù le.
  Although he didn't want to go, he ended up going.
- 虽然他家很有钱，可是他从来不浪费钱。
  Suīrán tā jiā hěn yǒuqián, kěshì tā cónglái bù làngfèi qián.
  Even though his family is rich, he never wastes money.
- 我妹妹虽然很胖，可是很灵活。
  Wǒ mèimei suīrán hěn pàng, kěshì hěn línghuó.
  Although my little sister is fat, she is flexible.

- 虽然 她准备得很好，但是 还是 有点紧张。
  Suīrán tā zhǔnbèi de hěn hǎo, dànshì háishì yǒudiǎn jǐnzhāng.
  Although she has prepared very well, she's still a little nervous.
- 你 虽然 学历高，可是 没有工作经验。
  Nǐ suīrán xuélì gāo, kěshì méiyǒu gōngzuò jīngyàn.
  Although you're well-educated, you don't have work experience.
- 奶奶 虽然 八十多岁了，但是 她精神很好。
  Nǎinai suīrán bāshí duō suì le, dànshì tā jīngshén hěn hǎo.
  Although grandma is in her eighties, she is energetic.
- 虽然 你们没有赢，但是 我知道大家尽力了。
  Suīrán nǐmen méiyǒu yíng, dànshì wǒ zhīdao dàjiā jìnlì le.
  Although you didn't win, I know that all of you did your best.
- 虽然 我认识他很长时间了，但是 我 还是 不了解他。
  Suīrán wǒ rènshi tā hěn cháng shíjiān le, dànshì wǒ háishì bù liǎojiě tā.
  Although I've known him for a long time, I still don't know him well.

Similar to

- A softer "but" with "buguo" (HSK4)
- Expressing "although" with "jinguan" (HSK4)
- Two words for "but" (HSK4)

Comparing "hui," "neng," "keyi"

The three modal verbs 会 (huì), 能 (néng), and 可以 (kěyǐ) are all often translated as "can" in English. Sometimes they are explained as: 会 means "know how to," 能 means "to be able to," and 可以 means "to have permission to." In reality, their usage does overlap somewhat.

Basic Meanings

The words 会, 能, and 可以 actually overlap a little in meaning. The first step is to understand their basic meanings, though:

- 会 can mean "know how to" and can express an action that you had to *learn* or *be trained in* to do.
- 能 means "to be able to" and expresses having a certain *ability* or having obtained a certain minimum *requirement*.
- 可以 means "may" or "to be allowed to" and expresses having another person's *permission*.

As for overlap, this graphic helps explain nicely:

The regions marked by letters are explained in the sections below:

- A: ability in the sense of "know how to" (会 is more common than 能)
- B: permission/request (use 能 or 可以)
- C: possibility (use 能 or 可以)
- D: permission not granted (use 不可以)
- E: impossibility (use 不能)

Expressing Ability

Both 会 and 能 can be used to express ability in something.

Structure

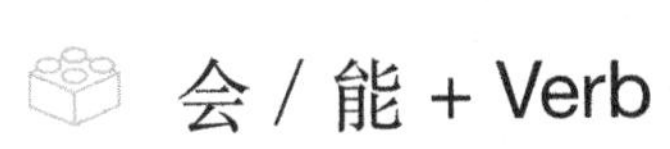

会 / 能 + Verb

Examples

- 我们都 会 游泳。

  Wǒmen dōu huì yóuyǒng.

  We all know how to swim.

- 他不 会 修电脑。

  Tā bù huì xiū diànnǎo.

  He doesn't know how to fix computers.

A: 你 会 说中文吗?

Nǐ huì shuō Zhōngwén ma?

Can you speak Chinese?

B: 不好意思，我只 会 说一点。

Bù hǎoyìsi, wǒ zhǐ huì shuō yīdiǎn.

Sorry, I can only speak a little.

A: 你 能 吃三碗米饭吗?

Nǐ néng chī sān wǎn mǐfàn ma?

Are you able to eat three bowls of rice?

B: 不 能 。

Bù néng.

I can't.

Expressing Permission

可以 is used to ask for or give permission. However, 能 can also be used to replace 可以 interchangeably.

Note: When a question is asked using 能 or 可以 it can be answered with 不能 or 不可以, meaning no, and only 可以 meaning yes. Chinese don't really answer with just 能 when it comes to permission.

Structure

Examples

A: 老师，我 可以 早点走吗?

Lǎoshī, wǒ kěyǐ zǎo diǎn zǒu ma?

Teacher, can I leave a little early?

B: 不可以。

Bù kěyǐ.

No, you can't.

A: 我 能 在这里抽烟吗?

Wǒ néng zài zhèlǐ chōuyān ma?

Can I smoke here?

B: 不 能 。

Bù néng.

No, you can't.

Expressing Possibility

能 and 可以 can also be used to express possibility.

Structure

Example

- 明天你 能 早点来吗?

  Míngtiān nǐ néng zǎodiǎn lái ma?

  Is it possible for you to come a little earlier tomorrow?

- 可不可以 换时间?

  Kě bu kěyǐ huàn shíjiān?

  Is it possible to change the time?

A: 外国人 能不能 参加?

Wàiguó rén néng bu néng cānjiā?

Is it possible for foreigners to attend?

B: 不 能 。

Bù néng.

Not possible.

Talking about the Future

Only 会 can be used to mean something is going to happen. It expresses that something in the future will happen and is often used to express trends or possibilities.

Structure

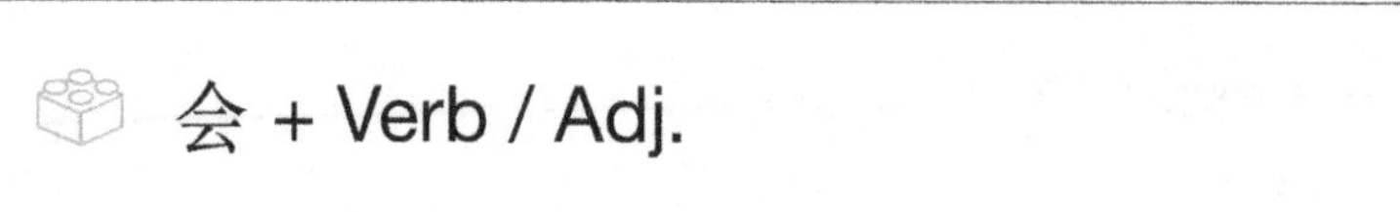

Examples

- 他不 会 跟你结婚。
  Tā bù huì gēn nǐ jiéhūn.
  He's not going to marry you.
- 你 会 生我的气吗?
  Nǐ huì shēng wǒ de qì ma?
  Will you be mad at me?
- 这样穿 会 好看吗?
  Zhèyàng chuān huì hǎokàn ma?
  Will I look good if I dress like this?

A: 今天 会 下雨吗?
Jīntiān huì xiàyǔ ma?
Is it going to rain today?

B: 我看不 会 。
Wǒ kàn bù huì.
I don't think it will.

Using Adverbs to Add Emphasis

By placing 很 (hěn) before 会, it adds emphasis to the level of ability and skill on the action presented. 很会 is commonly used to mean "to be good at" and expresses being very skillful at something, or doing something very well. It can be translated as "really know how to," as in "you really know how to speak Chinese!" Another way to put it is, "You are good at speaking Chinese."

When 很 is placed in front of 能, the meaning takes on a amazed/surprised tone on the action. Although more rarely used, it emphasizes quantity and amount. 很能 is most commonly used with 吃 (chī) to eat, and 睡 (shuì) to sleep. It's like the English equivalent of saying you "can really" do something. For example saying that someone "*can really* sleep" means that they can sleep a lot.

Note: 很可以 is not a phrase, and therefore this pattern does not apply to 可以.

Structure

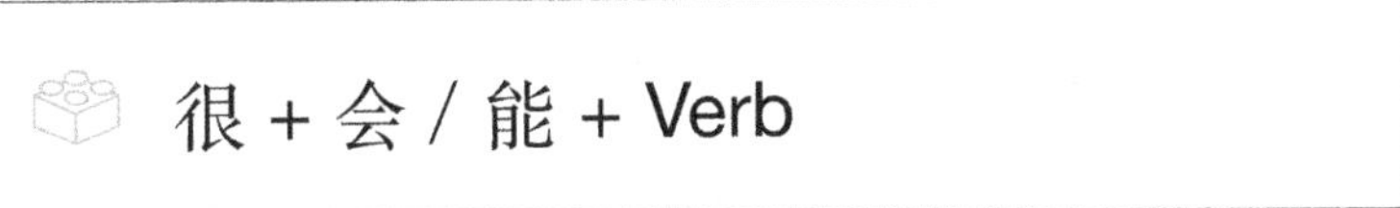

很 + 会 / 能 + Verb

Other degree adverbs like 真 (zhēn), 太 (tài), 这么 (zhème), etc. can also be used in place of 很.

Examples

- 他很能说。
  Tā hěn néng shuō.
  He's quite a talker.
- 我妈妈很会做饭。
  Wǒ māma hěn huì zuòfàn.
  My mother really knows how to cook.
  My mom cooks very well.
- 她才五岁，但是很会说话。
  Tā cái wǔ suì, dànshì hěn huì shuōhuà.
  She's only five but she's a smooth talker.
  The subject has good speaking skills.
- 这个女生很会打扮。
  Zhège nǚshēng hěn huì dǎban.
  This girl knows how to dress up really well.

Note that 很能说 means someone talks *a lot*, 很会说 means they *have a way with words*, but 很可以说 is just bad Chinese.

Examples used with other adverbs:

- 他太能睡了。
  Tā tài néng shuì le.
  He can really sleep.
  The subject can sleep a lot, for many hours.
- 你真能吃！
  Nǐ zhēn néng chī!
  Wow, you really can eat!
  The subject can eat a lot.
- 中国人真会吃！
  Zhōngguó rén zhēn huì chī!
  Chinese people can really eat.
  The subject has great knowledge about food and its culture, a true connoisseur.

- 没想到你 这么 能 吃苦。

  Méixiǎngdào nǐ zhème néng chīkǔ.

  I didn't expect you to be able to handle so much hardhsip.

Similar Expression with Different Meanings

- 我的脚好了，现在又 能 跳舞了。

  Wǒ de jiǎo hǎo le, xiànzài yòu néng tiàowǔ le.

  I am able to dance now since my foot is better. (The condition changed)

- 我学了两个月，现在我 会 跳舞了。

  Wǒ xué le liǎng gè yuè, xiànzài wǒ huì tiàowǔ le.

  I studied for two months. I know how to dance now. (It's a learned skill)

- 我爸妈同意了，现在我 可以 跳舞了。

  Wǒ bàmā tóngyì le, xiànzài wǒ kěyǐ tiàowǔ le.

  My parents agreed. I'm allowed to dance now. (Parents gave their permission)

Note that none of the three can be followed by the aspectual particle 过.

Similar to

- Expressing ability or possibility with "neng" (HSK1)
- Expressing permission with "keyi" (HSK2), page 108
- The use of Taiwanese Mandarin "hui" (HSK5)

Comparing "yao" and "xiang"

Both 要 (yào) and 想 (xiǎng) can essentially mean "want," but they can also be used in quite different ways, such as 想 (xiǎng) also meaning "to miss" when followed by a noun, and 要 (yào) also meaning "going to (do something)."

Followed by a Noun

Both 要 (yào) and 想 (xiǎng) may be followed by nouns, but pay attention to how the meaning of 想 (xiǎng) totally changes when used this way.

要 (yào) as "to Want"

Structure

In this pattern, 要 (yào) is directly followed by a thing (a noun), rather than by a verb. It is often used to buy something, or to order food at a restaurant.

It may be helpful to imagine a demanding child using this pattern to get stuff from his parents. This "*I want x!*" pattern can seem slightly impolite, but to the Chinese ear it's not as inherently rude as it may seem when translated directly into English. Tone of voice plays a key role when using this pattern in spoken Chinese.

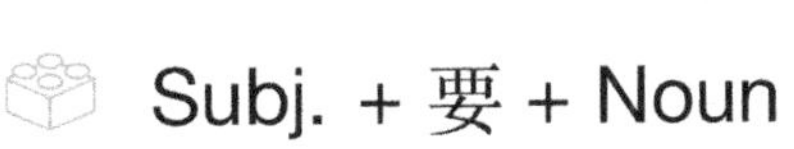

Examples

- 你也 要 茶吗? *ordering in a restaurant*
  Nǐ yě yào chá ma?
  Do you also want tea?
- 我们都 要 咖啡。 *ordering in a cafe*
  Wǒmen dōu yào kāfēi.
  We all want coffee.
- 大家 要 不 要 米饭? *ordering in a restaurant*
  Dàjiā yào bù yào mǐfàn?
  Does everyone want rice?
- 你们 要 冰水还是热水? *ordering in a restaurant*
  Nǐmen yào bīng shuǐ háishì rè shuǐ?
  Do you want ice water or hot water?

- 谢谢，我什么都不 要 。 *ordering in a restaurant*

  Xièxiè, wǒ shénme dōu bù yào.

  Thank you. I don't need anything.

想 (xiǎng) as "to Miss"

Pay attention here: unlike "想 (xiǎng) + Verb," the meaning of 想 (xiǎng) in the "想 (xiǎng) + Noun" pattern becomes "to miss."

Structure

Examples

- 我 想 你。

  Wǒ xiǎng nǐ.

  I miss you.

- 我有点 想 我的家人。

  Wǒ yǒudiǎn xiǎng wǒ de jiārén.

  I sort of miss my family.

- 你们回美国以后，会 想 中国菜吗?

  Nǐmen huí Měiguó yǐhòu, huì xiǎng Zhōngguó cài ma?

  Will you all miss Chinese food after you go back to the U.S.?

- 你女朋友不在的时候，你会 想 她吗?

  Nǐ nǚpéngyou bù zài de shíhou, nǐ huì xiǎng tā ma?

  Do you miss your girlfriend when she is not around?

- 妈妈打电话的时候跟我说，她很 想 我。

  Māma dǎ diànhuà de shíhou gēn wǒ shuō, tā hěn xiǎng wǒ.

  Mom called me and said she misses me a lot.

Followed by a Verb

要 (yào) and 想 (xiǎng) have similar meanings when followed by verbs. The difference is rather subtle, but 要 (yào) can sound more urgent or demanding (sometimes even childish), while 想 (xiǎng) is usually a bit more mature and polite. Tone of voice plays a big role here as well, though, so don't be afraid of offending people by using 要 (yào); the word itself isn't rude.

要 (yào) as "Want to"

Structure

It might help to think of 要 (yào) in this sense as meaning "want to" and 想 (xiǎng) as meaning "would like to."

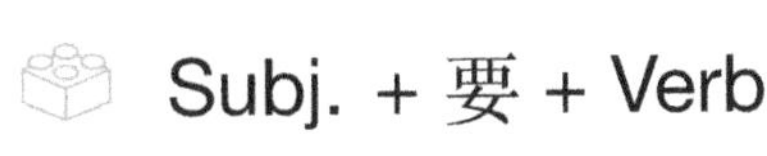

Examples

- 我 要 休息。
  Wǒ yào xiūxi.
  I want to rest.
- 你也 要 回家吗?
  Nǐ yě yào huíjiā ma?
  Do you also want to go home?
- 你们 要 喝什么?
  Nǐmen yào hē shénme?
  What do you want to drink?
- 我 要 帮老板做完这些工作。
  Wǒ yào bāng lǎobǎn zuò wán zhèxiē gōngzuò.
  I want to help the boss finish this work.
- 大家晚上 要 不 要 出去吃?
  Dàjiā wǎnshang yào bu yào chūqù chī?
  Does everyone want to go out to eat tonight?

想 (xiǎng) as "Would Like to"

Structure

It might help to think of 想 (xiǎng) as meaning "would like to" instead of "want to." In English, as well, "would like to" feels more indirect, and thus less demanding and more more polite.

Examples

- 你 想 去吗?
  Nǐ xiǎng qù ma?
  Would you like to go?
- 我不 想 见她。
  Wǒ bù xiǎng jiàn tā.
  I wouldn't like to see her.
- 周末你们 想 看电影吗?
  Zhōumò nǐmen xiǎng kàn diànyǐng ma?
  Would you like to see a movie this weekend?
- 我 想 请你吃饭。
  Wǒ xiǎng qǐng nǐ chīfàn.
  I'd like to treat you to dinner.
- 他们春节不 想 回家吗?
  Tāmen Chūnjié bù xiǎng huíjiā ma?
  Don't they want to go back home for Spring Festival?

要 (yào) as "Going to"

要 is used to indicate plans for the near future, much like "going to" in English. 想 (xiǎng) is not used in this way.

Structure

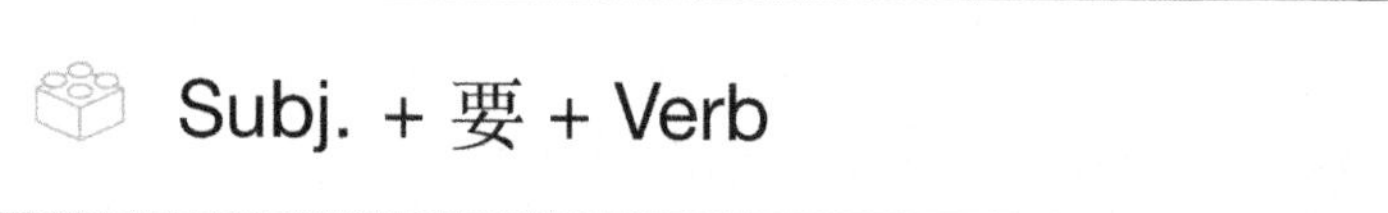

Examples

- 星期六我 要 去北京。
  Xīngqīliù wǒ yào qù Běijīng.
  I'm going to Beijing on Saturday.
- 下个月她 要 找新工作。
  Xià gè yuè tā yào zhǎo xīn gōngzuò.
  She is going to look for a new job next month.

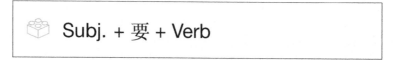

- 这个周末你们 要 出去玩吗?
  Zhège zhōumò nǐmen yào chūqù wán ma?
  Are you going out partying this weekend?
- 结婚以后，你 要 跟父母住在一起吗?
  Jiéhūn yǐhòu, nǐ yào gēn nǐ fùmǔ zhù zài yīqǐ ma?
  Are you going to live together with your parents after you get married?
- 生完孩子以后，你太太 要 回去工作吗?
  Shēng wán háizi yǐhòu, nǐ tàitai yào huíqù gōngzuò ma?
  Is your wife going back to work after she finishes giving birth to the baby?

想要 (xiǎngyào) as "Want"

Structure

You can put 要 (yào) and 想 (xiǎng) together to make the word 想要 (xiǎngyào), which means "to want." You can put either nouns or verbs after it.

 Subj. + 想要 + Noun / Verb

Examples

- 你 想要 几个孩子?
  Nǐ xiǎngyào jǐ gè háizi?
  How many kids do you want to have?
- 我老婆总是 想要 最贵的包。
  Wǒ lǎopo zǒngshì xiǎngyào zuì guì de bāo.
  My wife always wants the most expensive bags.
- 她 想要 找一个有钱的男朋友。
  Tā xiǎngyào zhǎo yī gè yǒuqián de nánpéngyou.
  She wants to find a rich boyfriend.
- 你们为什么 想要 离开北京?
  Nǐmen wèishénme xiǎngyào líkāi Běijīng?
  Why do you all want to leave Beijing?

- 他 想要 帮你找一个更好的工作。
  Tā xiǎngyào bāng nǐ zhǎo yī gè gèng hǎo de gōngzuò.
  He wants to help you find a better job.

Comparing "er" and "liang"

In Chinese, there are two words for "two." They are 二 (èr) and 两 (liǎng), and each is used in different circumstances.

Uses of 二 (èr)

二 (èr) is for Numbers

The digit "2" is 二 (èr). This is used generally in numbers, when counting to ten, giving out a phone number, and so on.

Unlike 两 (liǎng), 二 (èr) is not used to say there are "two" of something, and does not generally occur with measure words by itself. Numbers like 十二 (12) (shí'èr) and 二十二 (22) (èrshí-èr) end with a "2" and can still be combined with measure words. In those cases, 两 (liǎng) is not needed.

Examples

Here are some common examples of 二 (èr) in action:

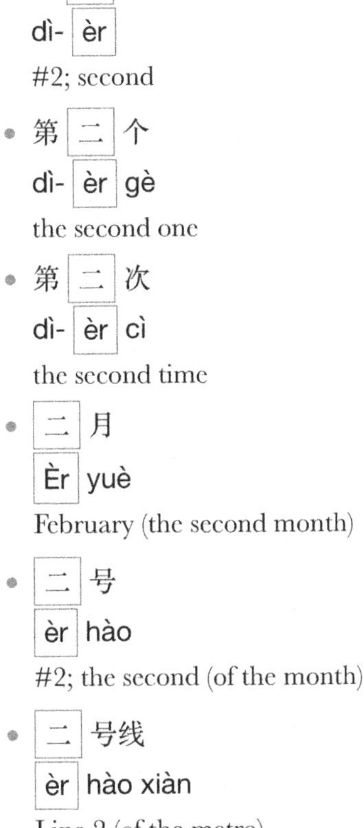

- 第二
  dì- èr
  #2; second
- 第二个
  dì- èr gè
  the second one
- 第二次
  dì- èr cì
  the second time
- 二月
  Èr yuè
  February (the second month)
- 二号
  èr hào
  #2; the second (of the month)
- 二号线
  èr hào xiàn
  Line 2 (of the metro)

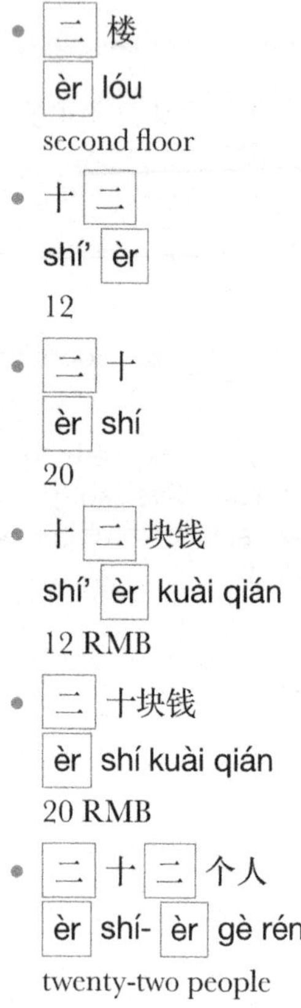

- 二楼
  èr lóu
  second floor
- 十二
  shí' èr
  12
- 二十
  èr shí
  20
- 十二块钱
  shí' èr kuài qián
  12 RMB
- 二十块钱
  èr shí kuài qián
  20 RMB
- 二十二个人
  èr shí- èr gè rén
  twenty-two people

Uses of 两 (liǎng)

两 (liǎng) is for Measure Words

When specifying quantities (and using measure words to do it), 两 (liǎng) is used. This is when you want to say "two of something" or "both."

Here are some common examples of 两 (liǎng) in action:

Examples

- 两个小时
  liǎng gè xiǎoshí
  two hours
- 两点
  liǎng diǎn
  2 o'clock
- 两天
  liǎng tiān
  two days

- 两 个星期
  liǎng gè xīngqī
  two weeks
- 两 个月
  liǎng gè yuè
  two months
- 两 年
  liǎng nián
  two years
- 两 次
  liǎng cì
  two times / twice
- 两 块钱
  liǎng kuài qián
  2 kuai / 2 RMB
- 两 百
  liǎng bǎi
  200

  note: 二百 (èrbǎi) is also acceptable.
- 两 千
  liǎng qiān
  2,000
- 我 两 个都要。
  Wǒ liǎng gè dōu yào.
  I want both of them.

Keyword Index

Look up grammar points based on keywords they contain.

Glossary

We strive to avoid unnecessarily technical terms on the Chinese Grammar Wiki, but occasionally it's sort of necessary, and sometimes even useful (yes, really!). So to help you out, we've placed all of the grammatical terms related to Mandarin Chinese in one place. Each term has a page on the wiki with a more complete description, and many pages also have lists of grammar points related to the term.

List of Mandarin Grammar Terms

Action verb — *Also known as: 动作动词 (dòngzuò dòngcí) and 行为动词 (xíngwéi dòngcí).* Action verbs describe what a subject did, is doing, or will do, physically.

Adjective — *Also known as: 形容词 (xíngróngcí).* Adjectives are the "describing" words of a language. In Chinese, they have some characteristics that they don't have in English.

Adjectival phrase — *Also known as: 形容词性词组 (xíngróngcí-xìng duǎnyǔ) and adjective phrase.* Adjectival phrases often consist of just an adjective and the adverbs modifying it, but they might also have other structures, such as an adjective and complement.

Adjectival predicate sentence — *Also known as: 形容词谓语句 (xíngróngcí wèiyǔ jù) and 形容词性谓语句 (xíngróngcí-xìng wèiyǔ jù).* A fancy name for a sentence where the predicate consists of an adjective.

Adverb — *Also known as: 副词 (fùcí).* Adverbs are words that modify verbs and adjectives. In Chinese, word order of adverbs is much stricter than in English. Chinese adverbs normally come before the main verb of a sentence, but in some cases come right at the beginning of a sentence.

Adverbial — *Also known as: 状语 (zhuàngyǔ).* An adverbial is a sentence element that functions like an adverb, modifying a verb or adjective.

Adverbial phrase — *Also known as: 副词短语 (fùcí duǎnyǔ) and adverb phrase.* An adverbial phrase is a phrase with two or more words that act like an adverb, modifying a verb or adjective.

Affirmative-negative question — *Also known as: 正反问句 (zhèng-fǎn wènjù) and alternative questions.* A common way to form questions in Chinese is to first use a verb in the positive, then repeat the same verb in its negative form, similar to how in English we can say, "Do you have money or not?" or "Have you or have you not been to the park?" This sentence pattern feels a lot more natural in Chinese than those admittedly awkward English equivalents, however.

Affix — *Also known as: 词缀 (cízhuì).* An affix is a linguistic unit added to the beginning, middle or end of a word to change its meaning (e.g. prefix, infix, suffix).

Aspect — *Also known as: 动作状态 (dòngzuò zhuàngtài).* Chinese does not use the concept of formal tenses. Instead, it employs what is called "grammatical aspect." Rather than conjugating its verbs, Chinese uses particles to indicate how a verb works within a particular timeframe, or how the verb relates to the flow of time. The particles most often used to indicate aspect in Chinese are 了 (le), 过 (guo), and 着 (zhe).

Aspectual particle — *Also known as: 动态助词 (dòngtài zhùcí).* These words are added to verbs to indicate aspect (not the same as tense). The particles most often used to indicate aspect in Chinese are 了 (le), 过 (guo), and 着 (zhe).

Attributive — *Also known as: 定语 (dìngyǔ).* An attributive is the word or phrase that directly precedes the noun it describes. Frequently it is linked to the noun with the structural particle 的 (de).

Auxiliary verb — *Also known as: modal verb, 助动词 (zhùdòngcí), 情态动词 (qíngtài dòngcí) and 能愿动词 (néngyuàn dòngcí).* Auxiliary verbs are "helping" verbs that come before main verbs and help express a tone or mood. (The word "modal" comes from "mood.") In English, auxiliary verbs include words like "should," "will," and "can," which all change something about the situation and the speaker's attitude. Auxiliary verbs express capability, possibility, necessity, obligation or willingness.

Cardinal number — *Also known as: 基数词 (jīshùcí).* Cardinal numbers are numbers such as 1, 2, or 3 used to indicate quantity. They contrast with ordinal numbers.

Causative verb — *Also known as: 使令动词 (shǐlìng dòngcí) and 使役动词 (shǐyì dòngcí).* A causative verb is a kind of verb that is used to indicate that someone or something causes something else to do or be something. In Chinese, 让 (ràng) is a major player in this space.

Complement — *Also known as: 补语 (bǔyǔ) and objective complement.* A complement is a word or phrase following a verb (or sometimes an adjective) that provides additional meaning to the verb phrase. Complements are not the same as objects, and can be as short as one character, or practically as long as a sentence. Complements provide additional information associated with verbs, such as degree, result, direction or possibility, and are extremely common. Complements are not a form of flattery (those are compliments); they're much more versatile than that!

Complex sentence — *Also known as: 复句 (fùjù).* A complex sentence is a sentence with one main clause and one or more subordinate clauses.

Conjunction — *Also known as: 连词 (liáncí).* Conjunctions in Chinese do exactly what they do in English: connect things. They help make the transition between ideas smoother and also show the relationships between those ideas.

Content word — *Also known as: 实词 (shící).* Content words refer to real objects in the real world, whether solid and palpable, or observable in some other way. These words refer to objects, actions, concepts, and even emotions, which exist in some real way as more than just grammatical tools. Words that serve purely grammatical roles are called function words.

Coverb — *Also known as: 副动词 (fùdòngcí) and 伴动词 (bàndòngcí).* A coverb is a verb that modifies the main verb of a sentence when used with its own object.

Degree adverb — *Also known as: 程度副词 (chéngdù fùcí) and adverb of degree.* Degree adverbs intensify or in some other way modify the degree of expression of the adjective (or verb).

Degree complement — *Also known as: 程度补语 (chéngdù bǔyǔ) and complement of degree.* While most complements follow verbs, degree complements can follow both verbs and adjectives. These complements intensify or modify the degree of expression of the verb or adjective.

Demonstrative pronoun — *Also known as: 指示代词 (zhǐshì dàicí).* A demonstrative pronoun is a pronoun used in the place of a noun and specifies what is being referred to.

Dependent clause — *Also known as: 从句 (cóngjù).* A dependent clause is dependent on and modifies an independent clause. Dependent clauses have a subject and verb, but also start with a subordinate conjunction, making it clear that they are not meant to stand on their own.

Direct object — *Also known as: 直接宾语 (zhíjiē bīnyǔ).* A direct object is what is being acted upon, thus receiving the action of a verb. In Chinese grammar, direct objects are often simply referred to as "objects."

Direction complement — *Also known as: 趋向补语 (qūxiàng bǔyǔ), directional complement and complement of direction.* A direction complement is a complement used to describe the direction of a verb. Verbs often already have some inherent movement implied, but by adding a direction complement, it becomes clearer where, exactly, that action is going.

Directional verb — *Also known as: 趋向动词 (qūxiàng dòngcí).* Directional verbs can be added to other verbs in a direction complement, illustrating which direction the verb is going.

Directional complement — See **direction complement**

Distinguishing word — *Also known as: 区别词 (qūbiécí) and attributive adjective.* "Distinguishing words" are rather foreign to the English speaker. On the surface they may seem like regular adjectives, but distinguishing words cannot have degree, so they cannot be modified by adverbs. Unlike normal adjectives, sentences involving distinguishing words use 是 (shì), and usually 的 (de) as well. Common words include the Chinese words for "male," "female," "real," "fake," and colors.

Existential verb — *Also known as: 存现动词 (cúnxiàn dòngcí).* Existential verbs declare the existence or nonexistence of things.

Function word — *Also known as: 虚词 (xūcí).* Function words do not refer to real objects in the real world; rather they serve purely grammatical roles in sentences, drawing relationships and logical connections between the content words in a sentence. Words that refer to real objects in the real world are called content words.

Judgment verb — *Also known as: 关系动词 (guānxì dòngcí) and 判断动词 (pànduàn dòngcí).* Judgment verbs are verbs used to express the speaker's judgment. This can be as simple as the verb "to be," but also covers a wide range of other verbs.

Indirect object — *Also known as: 间接宾语 (jiànjiē bīnyǔ).* Indirect objects occur when there are two objects in a sentence. The indirect object is for/to whom/what the action of the verb is done and who/what is receiving the direct object. In Chinese grammar, indirect objects are often referred to as second objects.

Independent clause — *Also known as: 主句 (zhǔjù).* An independent clause is a clause that has a subject and a predicate that modifies the subject, allowing it to stand alone as a sentence.

Independent phrase — *Also known as: 独立语 (dúlì yǔ).* An independent phrase has no subject acting out the verb in the sentence.

Interjection — *Also known as: 叹词 (tàncí) and 感叹词 (gǎntàncí).* This type of word is used in exclamations or various kinds of emotional response.

Interrogative pronoun — See **question word**

Intransitive verb — *Also known as: 不及物动词 (bùjíwù dòngcí).* Intransitive verbs are verbs which take no direct object.

Location word — *Also known as: 方位名词 (fāngwèi míngcí), 方位词 (fāngwèi cí) and noun of locality.* Location words are nouns showing direction and location.

Main clause — See **independent clause**

Measure word — *Also known as: 量词 (liàngcí) and classifier.* Measure words are used together with numerals to indicate the quantity of a noun, and sometimes even of an action. The general term for "measure word" in linguistics is "classifier," because measure words involve some kind of classification of the noun (or action) being counted.

Mimetic word — See **onomatopoeia**

Modal adverb — *Also known as: 语气副词 (yǔqì fùcí) and tone adverb.* Modal adverbs express likelihood with adverbs such as probably, possibly, evidently, certainly, etc.

Modal particle — *Also known as: 语气助词 (yǔqì zhùcí), 语气词 (yǔqì cí), Sentence-final particle and Sentential particle.* Modal particles are words used at the end of sentences to indicate mood, or attitude. They tend to be neutral tone and hard to translate, but they add a bit of "flavor" to a sentence. See also particles.

Modal verb — See **auxiliary verb**

Negative adverb — *Also known as: 否定副词 (fǒudìng fùcí).* Negative adverbs negate verbs and adjectives to make a negative statement. The main ones in Chinese are 不 (bù) and 没 (méi).

Noun — *Also known as: 名词 (míngcí).* You may have learned these as "person, place, or thing." Nouns often act as subjects, are modified by adjectives, and can be counted with measure words in Chinese.

Noun measure word — *Also known as: 名量词 (míngliàngcí) and nominal measure word.* As the name suggests, these are measure words that are only used for nouns.

Noun phrase — *Also known as: 名词性短语 (míngcí-xìng duǎnyǔ).* A noun phrase is a phrase with a noun or pronoun as a head word that has any sort of modifier.

Numeral — *Also known as: 数词 (shùcí).* A numeral is a symbol that represents a number.

Nominal predicate sentence — *Also known as: 名词谓语句 (míngcí wèiyǔjù).* Nominal predicate sentences are sentences with a noun phrase that functions as the main predicate of the sentence.

Object — *Also known as: 宾语 (bīnyǔ).* The object is the receiver of the action of the verb.

Onomatopoeia — *Also known as: 象声词 (xiàngshēngcí) and 拟声词 (nǐshēngcí).* Onomatopoeia are words which represent sounds and noises.

Ordinal number — *Also known as: 序数词 (xùshù cí).* Ordinal numbers are numbers used to express rank or sequence. Think "1st," "2nd," etc. Ordinal numbers contrast with cardinal numbers.

Particle — *Also known as: 助词 (zhùcí).* Particles are function words that depend on other words or phrases to impart meaning. They're kind of like prepositions, but more abstract. In Chinese, the key ones are aspectual particles (for indicating aspect), structural particles (for indicating relationships between words), and modal particles (for indicating mood). Chinese particles are also special words because they tend to always take the neutral tone.

Passive voice — *Also known as: 被动结构 (bèidòng jiégòu), 被动句式 (bèidòng jùshì), 被动语态 (bèidòng yǔtài) and the passive.* "Passive voice" is a grammatical term used to refer to sentences in which the "recipient" of an action (often referred to as the "direct object" or simply "object") becomes the subject of the sentence, and the "doer" of the action is demoted to secondary importance or omitted altogether.

Passive structure — See **passive voice**

Personal pronoun — *Also known as: 人称代词 (rénchēng dàicí).* Personal pronouns include 我 (wǒ), 你 (nǐ), 他 (tā), and 她 (tā). To make them plural, all you need to do is add the suffix -们 (-men) to them. There is also a polite second person form 您 (nín), which cannot normally take the -们 (-men) suffix.

Place noun — *Also known as: 处所名词 (chùsuǒ míngcí).* Place nouns are nouns describing the position or place of something.

Place adverb — *Also known as: 处所副词 (chùsuǒ fùcí), location adverb, adverb of place and adverb of location.* Place adverbs modify the location of a verbs or adjective.

Placement verb — See **existential verb**

Phrase — *Also known as: 短语 (duǎnyǔ) and 词组 (cízǔ).* A phrase is a group of words that expresses a concept. It can be focused on fleshing out a particular word, as in a noun phrase or verb phrase. See also clause, which expresses a more complete thought.

Possessive pronoun — *Also known as: 物主代词 (wùzhǔ dàicí).* Possessive pronouns take the place of a noun and show ownership.

Potential complement — Verbs can take potential complements to indicate whether or not an action is possible. Potential complements contain a 得 (de) or a 不 (bu) immediate after the verb being modified, and are quite common in everyday spoken Mandarin.

Predicate — *Also known as: 谓语 (wèiyǔ).* Predicates are the main verb or verb phrase of a sentence, and state something about the subject. Aside from verbs, adjectives and sometimes even nouns can be predicates as well.

Preposition — *Also known as: 介词 (jiècí).* Prepositions are words that indicate location or direction. They are called "pre"-positions because they are positioned *before* the words that they modify.

Prepositional phrase — *Also known as: 介词短语 (jiècí duǎnyǔ).* A prepositional phrase is a phrase beginning with a preposition that precedes the word it modifies and clarifies that word's relationship with another word in the sentence.

Pronoun — *Also known as: 代词 (dàicí).* Pronouns substitute in for regular nouns and proper nouns to avoid unnecessary repetition of the same words over and over again.

Proper noun — *Also known as: 专有名词 (zhuānyǒu míngcí).* A proper noun is specific person, place or thing. Proper nouns are generally capitalized (e.g. Anubis, Asgard, AllSet Learning), both in English and in pinyin.

Psychological verb — *Also known as: 心理动词 (xīnlǐ dòngcí) and psych verb.* A psychological verb is a verb that conveys the speaker's mental state or attitude.

Qualitative adjective — *Also known as: 性质形容词 (xìngzhì xíngróngcí).* Qualitative adjectives describe the quality or nature of something.

Quantitative phrase — *Also known as: 数量短语 (shùliàng duǎnyǔ).* Quantitative phrases express a measurement of amount.

Quantity complement — *Also known as: 数量补语 (shùliàng bǔyǔ), quantitative complement and complement of quantity.* A quantity complement follows a verb and supplies information regarding an amount.

Question pronoun — See **question word**

Question word — *Also known as: 疑问代词 (yíwèn dàicí), question pronoun, interrogative pronoun.* A **question word** refers to a special kind of pronoun used to ask questions. These would include 什么 (shénme), 什么时候 (shénme shíhou), 谁 (shéi), 哪儿 (nǎr) / 哪里 (nǎlǐ), 哪个 (nǎge), 为什么 (wèishénme), 怎么 (zěnme). Beginners should pay attention to the placement of question words.

Reduplication — It is one of the great ironies of linguistics that the term for repeating a word is overly repetitive itself. You'd think that the word "duplication" would work just fine, but the linguistic term really is reduplication. In Chinese, verbs and adjectives are often reduplicated.

Relational verb — See **judgment verb**

Result complement — *Also known as: 结果补语 (jiéguǒ bǔyǔ), complement of result, resultative complement and result compound.* Result complements are a kind of verbal complement that appears very frequently in Chinese. Surprisingly enough, they're used to describe the result of a verb.

Scope adverb — *Also known as: 范围副词 (fànwéi fùcí).* Scope adverbs modify and expand a verb or adjective.

Sentence with a nominal predicate — See **nominal predicate sentence**

Sentence with a verbal predicate — *Also known as: 动词谓语句 (dòngcí wèiyǔ jù).* A sentence with a verb as the main element of its predicate is called a sentence with a verbal predicate. This type of sentence is extremely common.

Sentence with an adjectival predicate — See **adjectival predicate sentence**

Sentence with a subject-predicate structure as predicate — *Also known as: 主谓谓语句 (zhǔ-wèi wèiyǔ jù).*

Sentence-final particle — See **modal particle**

Sentential particle — See **modal particle**

Separable verb — *Also known as: 离合词 (líhécí) and verb-object phrase.* "Separable verbs" get their name from their ability to "separate" into two parts (a verb part and an object part), with other words in between. In fact, you could also simply call separable verbs "verb-object phrases."

Subject — *Also known as: 主语 (zhǔyǔ).* A subject is a noun or pronoun that the sentence centers around. It is the actor of the verb and is what something is said about.

Subject-predicate construction — *Also known as: 主谓结构 (zhǔ-wèi jiégòu).* The subject-predicate construction consists of a subject and a predicate, and may be part of a larger sentence, or may serve as a sentence on its own.

Subject-predicate sentence — *Also known as: 主谓句 (zhǔ-wèi jù).* A sentence composed of a subject and a predicate. The vast majority of sentences fit this description.

Subordinate clause — See **dependent clause**

State complement — *Also known as: 状态补语 (zhuàngtài bǔyǔ), 情态补语 (qíngtài bǔyǔ) and complement of state.* State complements describe an achieved state of an action. State complements are usually adjective phrases (adverb + adjective) but can take the form of verb phrases, subject-predicate phrases, or other complements. State complements that are adjective phrases often look the same as degree complements and thus are often lumped together with degree complements in textbooks.

Stative adjective — *Also known as: 状态形容词 (zhuàngtài xíngróngcí).* A stative adjective is an adjective describing a relatively unchanging or permanent condition/state.

Stative verb — *Also known as: 状态动词 (zhuàngtài dòngcí), 静态动词 (jìngtài dòngcí), state verb and static verb.* A stative verb is a verb describing a relatively unchanging or permanent condition/state. Stative verbs in Mandarin are usually translated as adjectives in English.

Structural particle — *Also known as: 结构助词 (jiégòu zhùcí).* A structural particle is a function word that denotes the structural/grammatical relationship between elements of a sentence.

Time adverb — *Also known as: 时间副词 (shíjiān fùcí).* Adverbs of time express the when, how long, or how often of a verb.

Time phrase — *Also known as: 时间短语 (shíjiān duǎnyǔ).* A time phrase occurs before the verb phrase and indicates the when, how long, or how often of a situation.

Time noun — *Also known as: 时间名词 (shíjiān míngcí), 时间词 (shíjiāncí), time nominal and temporal noun.* Time nouns are nouns that provide information regarding time. One reason they're noteworthy in Chinese is that words indicating time in English are often adverbs, whereas their Chinese counterparts are nouns.

Time-measure complement — *Also known as: 时量补语 (shí-liàng bǔyǔ).* Time-measure complements show the state or duration of an action.

Tone adverb — See **modal adverb**

Topic-comment structure — *Also known as: 主题句 (zhǔtí-jù), 主题结构 (zhǔtí jiégòu), 主题评论结构 (zhǔtí-pínglùn jiégòu), 主题述题结构 (zhǔtí-shùtí jiégòu) and 主题评述结构 (zhǔtí-píngshù jiégòu).* A topic-comment structure is an alternative to the typical subject-predicate sentence structure, whereby a topic (or theme) is followed by the speaker's comment on that topic. The topic is not the "doer" (subject) of the sentence, but rather sets the scope of the comments (some thoughts related to the topic).

Transitive verb — *Also known as: 及物动词 (jíwù dòngcí).* A transitive verb is an verb which takes a direct object.

Verb — *Also known as: 动词 (dòngcí).* Verbs are the "action" words which make up the predicates of most sentences, but may also simply indicate relationships, changes, or mental activity rather than physical actions. Verbs may take objects, and can also be reduplicated in Chinese. They can be negated, as well as modified by particles.

Verb measure word – *Also known as: 动量词 (dòng liàngci), verbal measure word and verbal classifier.* A verb measure word accompanies the number of times a verb occurred to count the frequency or re-occurrence of an action. See: Measure words for verbs

Verb phrase – *Also known as: 动词性短语 (dòngcí-xìng duǎnyǔ) and verbal phrase.* A verb phrase is a phrase with a verb as a head word that has any sort of modifier. It commonly includes modal verbs before it and objects after it.

Verbal measure word – *Also known as: 动量补语 (dòng-liàng bǔyǔ), verb measure word, verbal classifier and action-measure complement.* This type of measure word is not used to count nouns. Rather, it is placed after verbs to show the frequency of an action.

Verbal predicate sentence – See **sentence with a verbal predicate**

Acknowledgments

The Chinese Grammar Wiki may have been pioneered by AllSet Learning, but it would not be possible without the hard work of many selfless individuals, including AllSet Learning interns, students, teachers, and regular users. Thank you!

AllSet Interns

• Donna Yee • Lucas Simons • Hugh Grigg • Greg McAndrews • Jonathan Pope • Pavel Dvorak • Parry Cadwallader • Jack Overstreet • Dan Emery • Erick Garcia • Mei Tong • Ben Slye • Brandon Sanchez • Logan Pauley • Ashlyn Weber • Michelle Birkenfeldt • Zach Herzog • Jazlyn Akaka • Salomé Vergne • Natalie Kuan • Jack Du • Erick Garcia • Cai Qingyang • Michael Moore • Liza Fowler • Mike Blood • Jacob Rodgers • Dominic Pote • Amani Core • Michelle Guerra • Amanda Gilbride • Callan Mossman • Jenna Salisbury • Audrey Brady • Jocelyn Kwong • Natalia Tun • Jake Liu

Volunteer Editors

Some of these editors did tons of work on their own, while others emailed in issues they found. We thank them all for the hard work and valuable contributions!

• Nicholas Fiorentini • Noémi Németh • Betsy • HuaWei • Kryby • Jay • Luolimao • Trackpick • Morris • Philip Harding • Gintaras Valentukonis • Benedikt Rauh

AllSet Teachers and Staff

• 马丽华 (Mǎ Lìhuá) • 李炯 (Lǐ Jiǒng) • 陈世霜 (Chén Shìshuāng) • 刘倖倖 (Liú Xìngxìng) • 赵以华 (Zhào Yǐhuá) • 于翠 (Yú Cuì) • 杨仁君 (Yáng Rénjùn) • 毛思平 (Máo Sīpíng) • 吴蒙蒙 (Wú Méngméng) • 贾贝茜 (Jiǎ Bèixī) • Parry Cadwallader • Michael Moore • John Pasden

Big props also go to full-time staff 李炯 (Lǐ Jiǒng) and 马丽华 (Mǎ Lìhuá) for their unflinching dedication to repeated proofreading tasks as we completed the final checks of the print book.

Sincere thanks to Parry Cadwallader for making both the original wiki itself as well as the ebook version of the Chinese Grammar Wiki possible technically, with very little extra production work needed from the academic team. A big thank you also to Adam Abrams for all the layout work that went into creating the print version.

Other Credits

The Chinese Grammar Wiki website and ebook both make use of the **Silk** icon set **FamFamFam.com**. The Chinese Grammar Wiki BOOK (print edition) uses a "structure" icon from **Pixeden.com**, as well as several icons from **Icomoon.io**. The HSK Grammar series uses graphics from Pablo Stanley's outstanding **Humaaans** vector art library.

References

This page is a bibliography for the Chinese Grammar Wiki. It lists all sources referenced extensively when researching the content of the Chinese Grammar Wiki grammar points.

- Chen, Ru 陈如, and Xiaoya Zhu 朱晓亚. *Hanyu Changyong Geshi 330 Li 汉语常用格式 330 例 [Common Chinese Patterns 330]*. Beijing: Beijing Foreign Languages Printing House, 2010. Print.
- Fang, Yuqing 房玉清. *Shiyong Hanyu Yufa 实用汉语语法 [A Practical Chinese Grammar]*. Beijing: Beijing Yuyan Daxue Chubanshe, 2008. Print.
- General Information on the HSK. *Hanyu Kaoshi Fuwu Wang*, http://www.chinesetest.cn. Web.
- Herzberg, Qin Xue, and Larry Herzberg. *Basic Patterns of Chinese Grammar: A Student's Guide to Correct Structures and Common Errors*. Berkeley, CA: Stone Bridge, 2011. Print.
- Ho, Yong. *Intermediate Chinese*. New York: Hippocrene, 2004. Print.
- Jiang Liping 姜丽萍, ed. Wang Fang 王芳, Wang Feng 王枫, and Liu Liping 刘丽萍. *标准课程 Standard Course: HSK 1*. Beijing: Beijing Language and Culture University Press, 2014. Print.
- Jiang Liping 姜丽萍, ed. Wang Feng 王枫, Liu Liping 刘丽萍, and Wang Fang 王芳. *标准课程 Standard Course: HSK 2*. Beijing: Beijing Language and Culture University Press, 2014. Print.
- Jiang Liping 姜丽萍, ed. Yu Miao 于淼, and Li Lin 李琳. *标准课程 Standard Course: HSK 3*. Beijing: Beijing Language and Culture University Press, 2014. Print.
- Jiang Liping 姜丽萍, ed. Dong Zheng 董政 and Zhang Jun 张军. *标准课程 Standard Course: HSK 4 上*. Beijing: Beijing Language and Culture University Press, 2014. Print.
- Jiang Liping 姜丽萍, ed. Zhang Jun 张军 and Dong Zheng 董政. *标准课程 Standard Course: HSK 4 下*. Beijing: Beijing Language and Culture University Press, 2014. Print.
- Jiang Liping 姜丽萍, ed. Liu Chang 刘畅 and 鲁江 Lu Jiang. *标准课程 Standard Course: HSK 5 上*. Beijing: Beijing Language and Culture University Press, 2014. Print.
- Jiang Liping 姜丽萍, ed. 鲁江 Lu Jiang and Liu Chang 刘畅. *标准课程 Standard Course: HSK 5 下*. Beijing: Beijing Language and Culture University Press, 2015. Print.
- Jiang Liping 姜丽萍, ed. Yao Shujun 么书君 and Yang Huizhen 杨慧真. *标准课程 Standard Course: HSK 6 上*. Beijing: Beijing Language and

Culture University Press, 2015. Print.

- Jiang Liping 姜丽萍, ed. Yang Huizhen 杨慧真 and Yao Shujun 么书君. *标准课程 Standard Course: HSK 6 下*. Beijing: Beijing Language and Culture University Press, 2016. Print.
- Li, Charles N., and Sandra A. Thompson. *Mandarin Chinese: A Functional Reference Grammar*. Berkeley: U of California, 1981. Print.
- Li, Dejin 李德津, and Meizhen Cheng 程美珍, eds. *Waiguoren Shiyong Hanyu Yufa 外国人实用汉语语法 [A Practical Chinese Grammar for Foreigners]*. Beijing: Beijing Yuyan Daxue Chubanshe, 1998. Print.
- Li, Luxing 李禄兴, Ling Zhang 张玲, and Juan Zhang 张娟. *Hanyu Yufa Baixiang Jianglian: Chuzhongji 汉语语法百项讲练：初中级 [Chinese Grammar–Broken Down Into 100 Items]*. Beijing: Beijing Language and Culture UP, 2011. Print.
- Li, Xiaoqi 李晓琪, ed. *Xiandai Hanyu Xuci Shouce 现代汉语虚词手册 [Modern Chinese Function Words Handbook]: A Guide to Function Words in Modern Chinese*. Beijing: Beijing Daxue Chubanshe, 2003. Print.
- Liu, Delian 刘德联, and Xiaoyu Liu 刘晓雨. *Hanyu Kouyu Changyong Jushi Lijie 汉语口语常用句式例解 [Exemplification of Common Sentence Patterns in Spoken Chinese]*. Ed. Liwen Song 宋立文. Beijing: Beijing Daxue Chubanshe, 2005. Print.
- Liu, Xun 刘珣, ed. *Xin Shiyong Hanyu Keben 新实用汉语课本 [New Practical Chinese Reader Textbook 1]*. Beijing: Beijing Language and Culture UP, 2002. Print.
- Liu, Xun 刘珣. *Xin Shiyong Hanyu Keben 新实用汉语课本 [New Practical Chinese Reader Textbook 2]*. Beijing: Beijing Language and Culture UP, 2002. Print.
- Liu, Xun 刘珣. *Xin Shiyong Hanyu Keben 新实用汉语课本 [New Practical Chinese Reader Textbook 3]*. Beijing: Beijing Language and Culture UP, 2003. Print.
- Liu, Yuehua 刘月华, Wenyu Pan 潘文娱, and Wei Gu 故桦. *Shiyong Xiandai Hanyu Yufa 实用现代汉语语法 [Practical Modern Chinese Grammar]*. Beijing: Shangwu Yinshuguan Chuban, 2001. Print.
- Liu, Yuehua, and Tao-chung Yao. *Zhongwen Tingshuo Duxie 中文听说读写 [Integrated Chinese Textbook Simplified Characters Level 1 Part 2]*. 3rd ed. Boston: Cheng & Tsui, 2009. Print.
- Liu, Yuehua, and Tao-chung Yao. *Zhongwen Tingshuo Duxie 中文听说读写 [Integrated Chinese Textbook Simplified Characters Level 2 Part 2]*. 3rd ed. Boston: Cheng & Tsui, 2009. Print.
- Liu, Yuehua, and Tao-chung Yao. *Zhongwen Tingshuo Duxie 中文听说读写 [Integrated Chinese Textbook Simplified Characters Level 1 Part 1]*.